MW01254732

Are You the One Who Was to Come?

Commentary on the Epistle to the Hebrews

Dr. Arthur C. Woods

Are You the One Who Was to Come?
by Arthur C. Woods

Printed in the United States of America

Library of Congress Control Number: 2003091651
ISBN 1-591605-31-8

Xulon Press
www.xulonpress.com

To order additional copies, call 1-866-909-BOOK (2665).

Dedication

This book is dedicated to my wife, Laurie, and my three Children: Chuck, Andrew and Lauren, each of whom was an encouragement in the writing of this book as well as an encouragement in my life and ministry.

I also thank the students of Lancaster Bible College for their persistent urging that this book go to press and the church family at Hanover Evangelical Free Church for giving me the time to dedicate to this effort.

Special thanks to my secretary, June Shoff, for her tireless efforts in typing and correcting this manuscript and to Tom Sager, Andrew Woods and Laurie Woods for their proof-reading and content suggestions.

Author's Preface

There already exist more commentaries on the Epistle to the Hebrews than anyone is likely to read in a lifetime, yet I am motivated to make a contribution to the field. Many of the interpretations within this volume are unique in that they have been driven by a strong commitment to the audience of Hebrews being Jews saved under the Old Covenant. This approach sets this work apart from the field and results in many new thoughts on the so-called difficult passages.

An important aspect of this commentary is the outline imbedded in its chapter titles and subtitles. They are designed to reflect the flow of the book of Hebrew and function to demonstrate how each section supports the argument that Jesus is the one who was to come.

As with all commentaries, this is not an inspired work. Its arguments and logic must be prayerfully evaluated in light of the Scriptures. While attempting to be faithful to the Word, humility demands that I acknowledge the vulnerability of new ideas and the possibility of future light clarifying difficult issues.

It is my prayer that this commentary contribute to the

mix of ideas on Hebrews and provoke thinking outside traditional understanding of this powerful book of Scripture. Perhaps those, whose theological understanding and scholarship exceed mine, will be motivated to research this approach to Hebrews for themselves and subsequently produce their own written work on the subject. May the Lord use this book for his glory, as he sees fit!

Contents

ix

Chapter One

Jesus is the One Who was to Come, An Introduction to Hebrews

Overview

The name Hebrews is the only identification of the intended audience of this great book and there is no identification of its author. The letter does, however, have a number of details that can shed some light on these issues.

The book is clearly written to a Jewish audience who is suffering persecution at the hands of Rome and who is actively participating in worship in the temple of Jerusalem. The description of persecution in chapter ten, verses 32 to 34, cause some to postulate that the book was written to Christians suffering under the hand of the Roman Emperor Nero. This does not, however, have to be the conclusion.

There was significant persecution of the Jews throughout the first-century. The Emperor Claudius who reigned from 41 AD to 54 AD is reported in Acts 18, verse two, as the one who issued an edict for all Jews to leave Rome. His successor, Nero, reigning from 54 AD to 68 AD, persecuted and provoked the Jews sufficiently that they rebelled and began the Jewish War in 66 AD. Prior to the war Judah was ruled by Roman procurators. Biblical accounts speak of Felix who was succeeded by Festus. Josephus reports that Festus was followed by Albinus who he described as one who "...abused his authority over those about him, in order to plunder those that lived quietly." Josephus also described his successor, Florus, as the wickedest of all the Roman procurators of Judea and the immediate occasion of the Jewish war. (Josephus p 167) Persecution of the Jews throughout the first-century leading up to the Jewish wars is a well-documented fact.

This is significant because this commentary takes the position that Hebrews was written to a Jewish, non-Christian, audience. Most commentators believe Hebrews was written to Jewish Christians. The author's use of the term "brothers" is frequently cited as evidence of his "Christian" brotherhood with them. It could, however, just as easily be an expression of his "Jewish" brotherhood with them. This approach to their brotherhood would be further strengthened if these were not simply Jews by birth, but rather zealous Jews believing God's promises to Abraham that he would send a Messiah.

It is the position of this commentary that the letter of Hebrews was written to Jews saved under the old covenant by faith in the coming Messiah. The beginning chapters of this commentary will catalog some of those Old Testament saints who demonstrate that their salvation came from a fervent belief in a Messiah who would save them.

The purpose of the book of Hebrews was to ~~convenience~~ Convince Old Testament saints saved under the old covenant, by faith in a coming Messiah, to believe that Jesus was the Messiah who was to come. The focus of the book is on demonstrating that Jesus is the Messiah.

Author & Intended Audience

The author of Hebrews does not identify himself in the text. Throughout this commentary the expression "the author of Hebrews" will be used rather than any specific name. Inasmuch as the Holy Spirit did not see fit to retain the name of the author in the text, it is prudent that one not be overly dogmatic in his position on authorship.

The argument for Pauline authorship around the year 64 AD is a good one. Hebrews may well have been Paul's last book, written from prison in Rome, just before his death which is traditionally described as execution by the Roman Emperor Nero.

The text says in Hebrews 13:24, "Those from Italy greet you." This would lead one to believe that the book was written from Rome. This positions Paul, a prisoner in Rome, as the likely author. Some have argued that the letter was written to Rome and the greeting was from former citizens of Italy wanting to be remembered to their friends at Rome. This does not seem likely, particularly since there was not a large Jewish community in Rome. The book of Acts chapter 18 had already made the point that the Jews were banned from Rome under the Emperor Claudius. There would be little reason to send this letter to Rome.

It is far more likely that the apostle Paul, writing from Rome, wrote to an extensive Jewish community such as existed in Judea. There is no question, however, that the letter was prepared for wider distribution in hopes that everyone would hear of the Messiah who had come.

Another argument for Pauline authorship can be made from Peter's statement in 2 Peter 3:15 & 16:

> "Bear in mind that our Lord's patience means salvation, just as our dear brother Paul also wrote to you with the wisdom that God gave him. He writes the same way in all his letters, speaking in them of these matters. His letters contain some things that are hard to understand, which ignorant and unstable people distort, as they do the other Scriptures, to their own destruction."

Peter here reveals that he and Paul had similar audiences. He also concluded that Paul's writings were Scripture. In Peter's introduction to his two volume epistle he says he is writing to those in Pontus, Galatia, Cappadocia, Asia and Bithyna. None of the epistles attributed to Paul are directed to a general audience such as described here. If however Paul is the author of Hebrews, the book could certainly have included these places in its general circulation.

Among the church fathers, Clement of Rome, Clement of Alexander, and Eusebius all have writings that attribute the authorship of Hebrews to Paul. It is true that there was early controversy about the authorship of Hebrews. The eastern church was faster to embrace Pauline authorship than was the western church. This would be understandable if the letter came to and was circulated in the east. Its authorship in the west, that is Rome, would receive far less notoriety. This would be particularly true if the book was written by a prisoner like Paul. It is likely that Paul sent the letter with Timothy when Timothy was released from the Roman prison. (Heb 13:23) This may even explain why Paul did not identify himself in his writing. Timothy's life may have been at risk if he were carrying a letter from Paul, the notorious prisoner of Rome who would shortly be executed. Both the eastern and western churches eventually included Hebrews in the Canon and attributed authorship to the apostle Paul.

With the rise of textual criticism, Pauline authorship has come under fire in recent times. Proponents say that the style of Hebrews is too different from the other letters written by Paul. Differences, however, can be explained by comparing the intended audience of Paul's letters. If Hebrews was authored by him, it is the only letter written to an exclusively Jewish audience. It is quite likely that his choice of vocabulary and style would be altered to fit his audience. There is also a suggestion that Paul originally wrote this letter in Aramaic and that it was subsequently translated into Greek by Luke. This would further explain stylistic and vocabulary differences. A Biblical argument for the different styles could be made by comparing two of Paul's speeches. His message to the members of the synagogue at Piscidia Antioch of Acts 13:16-41 was far different than what he delivered to the Areopagus of Athens in Acts 17:23-31. Paul's education and training under Gamaliel (Acts 23:3) and his experience as a Pharisee and member of the Sanhedrin would certainly qualify him to be the author of a polished work on the intricacies of the religious practices of the Jews.

Paul's passion for the conversion of his Hebrew brothers is clearly in view in Romans 9, 10 & 11, particularly the third verse of Romans 9:

> For I could wish that I myself were cursed
> and cut off from Christ for the sake of my
> brothers, those of my own race,

Paul describes the people of Israel as his brothers. This is consistent with the book of Hebrews that frequently refers to the Hebrews as the author's brothers.

While the arguments for Paul are compelling, they are not infallible. Suggestions such as Apollos, Barnabas and Luke abound. It will be left to other commentators to make the case for those choices.

It is important to understand that regardless of authorship at the human level the inspiration of the Holy Spirit was at work. The understanding of the book is not impacted to any great extent by its author. On the other hand, the intended audience has a great impact on one's understanding of the book.

If one concludes that Hebrews was written to Christians, passages will be interpreted in that light. If however one believes that Hebrews was written to Jews saved under the old covenant, passages will be interpreted in that light. It has been the experience of the author of this commentary that those who believe Hebrews was written to Christians have great difficulty with a number of passages. Theological beliefs about eternal security and loss of salvation collide with the simple reading of some passages. No such collision and conflict occurs if one understands that Hebrews is written to non-Christian Jews. These Jews were saved under the old covenant by belief in the coming Messiah. Hebrews was written to convince them that Jesus was the Messiah who had come, and that they should move their faith from the promise of a Messiah to the reality of Jesus. Once this is understood and accepted the flow of Hebrews becomes very natural and there are no "difficult passages."

Date

The author was certainly writing before the destruction of the temple in 70 AD. This is clear from his descriptions of worship at the temple and priestly activity, that were going on at the time of his writing. Some have concluded that the book was written as late as 68 AD. While the earliest date of Hebrews cannot be firmly established an argument could be made that it was written before the Jewish War in 66 AD. A date as early as 64 AD would certainly be possible. This would coincide with the possibility of Pauline authorship.

Chapter Two

Jesus is the Source of Salvation for the Hebrews

Jesus is the Fulfillment of all Scripture Concerning the Redeemer (Luke 24:13-27)

13 ¶ Now that same day two of them were going to a village called Emmaus, about seven miles from Jerusalem. 14 They were talking with each other about everything that had happened. 15 As they talked and discussed these things with each other, Jesus himself came up and walked along with them; 16 but they were kept from recognizing him. 17 He asked them, "What are you discussing together as you walk along?" They stood still, their faces downcast. 18 One of them, named Cleopas, asked him, "Are you only a visitor to Jerusalem and do not know the things that have happened there in these days?" 19 "What things?" he asked. "About Jesus of Nazareth," they replied. "He was a prophet, powerful in word and deed before God and all the people. 20 The chief priests and our rulers handed him over to be sentenced to death, and they crucified him; 21 but we had hoped that he was the one who was going to redeem Israel. And what is more, it is the third day since all this took place. 22 In addition, some of our women amazed us. They went to the tomb early this morning 23 but didn't find his body. They came and told us that they had seen a vision of angels, who said he was alive. 24 Then some of our companions went to the tomb and found it just as the women had said, but him they did not see." 25 He said to them, "How foolish you are, and how slow of heart to believe all that the prophets have spoken! 26 Did not the Christ have to suffer these things and then enter his glory? 27 And beginning with Moses and all the Prophets, he explained to them what was said in all the Scriptures concerning himself.

On the same day Jesus was resurrected from the dead, two disciples were walking to a village called Emmaus. Jesus met them on the road and they walked along together. The conversation that ensued provided important insights into understanding the expectation of salvation in the Jewish mind of Jesus' day and the ability of Old Testament Scripture to inform and clarify those expectations.

The two disciples were unaware that they were speaking to Jesus. They discussed the events of the weekend including the crucifixion of Jesus of Nazareth, who they described as a prophet powerful in word and deed. They were downcast because they had hoped that he was the one who was going to redeem Israel. This statement demonstrates that the expectation was that a person (the Messiah) would redeem Israel. The disciples and others in Jesus' day were looking for redemption to come from an individual not a sacrificial system or obedience to the law of Moses.

It is likely that some, including the Pharisees, sought salvation through careful obedience to the law but others understood that salvation would come only through the Messiah.

This is a major topic in this commentary, for this author believes the book of Hebrews was written to convince the Jews who were waiting for a Messiah that Jesus was the one who was to come.

The discussion that Jesus had, with the Emmaus bound disciples, included explaining to them what was said in all the Scriptures concerning himself. Jesus was not seeking the disciples' obedience to the commands of Scripture; rather he was seeking their understanding that he was the Messiah spoken of in Scripture. In a previous conversation that Jesus had with a group of Jews trying to kill him for claiming equality with God, he rebuked them saying:

> You diligently study the Scriptures because you think that by them you possess eternal life. These are the Scriptures that testify about me, yet you refuse to come to me to have life. (John 5:39-40)

In the account of the conversation, on the road to Emmaus, Luke reports that Jesus began with Moses and the prophets but that he dealt with all Scripture. The discussion of Jesus in the Old Testament includes prophecies, types, patterns, illusions, etc. References to the Messiah are found in every genre of material including psalms, prophecy, legal material, and apocalyptic prophecy.

It is important to the understanding of the book of Hebrews that one thoroughly comprehends and agrees that salvation in the Old Testament came via faith in the Messiah who was to come. The remainder of this chapter will examine some of the major prophecies of the Old Testament in order to demonstrate that salvation and the redemption of Israel were to come through a person. Today we know that person to be Jesus.

Jesus is the Seed of the Woman Promised to Defeat Satan   (Genesis 3:14-15)

14 ¶ So the LORD God said to the serpent, "Because you have done this, "Cursed are you above all the livestock and all the wild animals! You will crawl on your belly and you will eat dust all the days of your life. 15 And I will put enmity between you and the woman, and between your offspring and hers; he will crush your head, and you will strike his heel."

The earliest recorded promise of a redeemer occurs in

Genesis, chapter three. Adam and Eve had sinned by eating of the fruit of the tree of the knowledge of good and evil. This action on their part resulted in a break in fellowship with God. They hid from him. God judged their sinful action by expelling them from the garden and prohibiting them from eating of the tree of life. Along with his judgment of their sin God promised their redemption. The promise was in its embryonic state when he said, "And I will put enmity between you and the woman and between your offspring and hers; he will crush your head, and you will strike his heel." This quotation from Genesis 3:15 speaks of a seed of the woman that would defeat Satan who was the power behind the serpent in the garden. The promised seed is described with the pronoun "he." This identified the one who was to come as one male individual. This embryonic promise, referred to as the protoevangelon, is expanded throughout Scripture and eventually the book of Hebrews makes it absolutely clear that Jesus is the one who was to come, the one who fulfils the prophecy of Genesis 3:15.

Jesus is the Seed of Abraham
Promised to be a Great Nation (Genesis 15:1-6)

1 ¶ After this, the word of the LORD came to Abram in a vision: "Do not be afraid, Abram. I am your shield, your very great reward." 2 ¶ But Abram said, "O Sovereign LORD, what can you give me since I remain childless and the one who will inherit my estate is Eliezer of Damascus?" 3 And Abram said, "You have given me no children; so a servant in my household will be my heir." 4 Then the word of the LORD came to him: "This man will not be your heir, but a son coming from your own body will be your heir." 5 He took him outside and said, "Look up at the heavens and count the stars—if indeed you can count them." Then he said to him, "So shall your offspring be." 6 Abram believed the LORD, and he credited it to him as righteousness.

In Genesis, chapter twelve, God called Abram to leave his country and go to a land that God would show him. He promised that he would give to Abram land, seed, and blessing. Abram, who had no children at the time, was promised offspring as numerous as the stars in the sky. There was, however, one offspring, to come from his own body, that was a special fulfilment of God's promise. In the short-term, that promise was fulfilled in the person of Abram's son Isaac. Abram, whose name meant "exalted father," had his name changed by God to Abraham which means, "father of many."

In Paul's New Testament letter to the Galatians, he adds clarity to God's promise of a seed to Abraham. He says in Galatians 3:16:

> "The promises were spoken to Abraham and to his seed. The Scripture does not say, 'and to seeds,' meaning many people, but 'and to your seed' meaning one person, who is Christ." (Gal 3:16)

Paul thereby identified that the seed of Abraham was Jesus. Paul continues in Galatians to establish the fact that:

> "If you belong to Christ, then you are Abraham's seed, and heirs according to the promise." (Gal 3:29)

Salvation in Paul's day came from faith in the seed of Abraham. Likewise, salvation in Abraham's day came from faith in the seed of Abraham that was to come.

Jesus is the Lion of Judah
Promised to Jacob's Son   (Genesis 49:8-12)

8 ¶ "Judah, your brothers will praise you; your hand will be on the neck of your enemies; your father's sons will bow down to you. 9 You are a lion's cub, O Judah; you return from the prey, my son. Like a lion he crouches and lies down, like a lioness— who dares to rouse him? 10 The sceptre will not depart from Judah, nor the ruler's staff from between his feet, until he comes to whom it belongs and the obedience of the nations is his. 11 He will tether his donkey to a vine, his colt to the choicest branch; he will wash his garments in wine, his robes in the blood of grapes. 12 His eyes will be darker than wine, his teeth whiter than milk."

As one works through the remaining chapters of the book of Genesis, one notes that the promised seed of Abraham becomes the promised seed of his son Isaac and then the promised seed of Isaac's son Jacob. At the end of Jacob's life, recorded in Genesis 49, he blessed his twelve children. These blessings included prophetic messages. Within the prophecies of these blessings one finds a particular promise to Jacob's son Judah. Jacob says:

> "The sceptre will not depart from Judah, nor the ruler's staff from between his feet, until he comes to whom it belongs and the obedience of the nations is his. He will tether his donkey to a vine, his colt to the choicest branch; he will wash his garments in wine, his robes in the blood of grapes. His eyes will be darker than wine, his teeth whiter than milk." (Gen 49:10-12)

This prophetic utterance, regarding Judah, expands

one's understanding of the nature of the seed to come. He would descend from the tribe of Judah and would be the ruler for all time. He would be the one who would triumph at the end of the age, as prophesied in the book of Revelation:

> Then one of the elders said to me, "Do not weep! See, the Lion of the tribe of Judah, the Root of David, has triumphed. He is able to open the scroll and its seven seals." (Rev 5:5)

The Messiah to come would have to prove his heritage to be from the tribe of Judah.

Jesus is the Prophet like Himself
Promised to Moses (Deuteronomy 18:15-19)

15 ¶ The LORD your God will raise up for you a prophet like me from among your own brothers. You must listen to him. 16 For this is what you asked of the LORD your God at Horeb on the day of the assembly when you said, "Let us not hear the voice of the LORD our God nor see this great fire any more, or we will die." 17 The LORD said to me: "What they say is good. 18 I will raise up for them a prophet like you from among their brothers; I will put my words in his mouth, and he will tell them everything I command him. 19 If anyone does not listen to my words that the prophet speaks in my name, I myself will call him to account.

At the time of the death of Jacob, his family was in Egypt. Subsequent to his death, the family grew in number and was eventually placed in bondage, under the control of the Egyptian nation. After four hundred years of slavery, God sent a deliverer named Moses to lead the Israelites out of Egypt to the land that God had promised Abraham in

Genesis, chapter twelve. Hebrews 11:26 clarifies that Moses believed in a coming Messiah. It says that he (Moses) suffered disgrace for the sake of Christ.

The descendants of Jacob, now called Israel, became a nation and were given an extensive law code, by God, at Mount Sinai. After forty years of wandering in the wilderness, the nation was on the verge of entering the promised land. At that time Moses recounted their travels, reminded them of their place in God's plan and described the future in the land. In Deuteronomy 18, Moses prophesied that the Lord would send to them a prophet like unto himself. They were to listen to him.

This prophet like unto Moses is the Messiah. Moses, described as a prophet, was also the leader of Israel. In a sense, the offices of king and prophet were combined in Moses. Throughout the subsequent history of Israel, the kingly office and the prophetic office were separated. Israel's prophets never served as king so none were ever quite like Moses. The prophet like unto Moses must hold the office of king as well as prophet. The Messiah would hold both offices as well as the office of Priest. The redemption of Israel and the salvation of its people would be tied up in the coming of the Messiah, who is the prophet like unto Moses.

Jesus is the King to Sit on the Throne Forever Promised to David   (2 Samuel 7:11b-16)

11 "*The LORD declares to you that the LORD himself will establish a house for you: 12 When your days are over and you rest with your fathers, I will raise up your offspring to succeed you, who will come from your own body, and I will establish his kingdom. 13 He is the one who will build a house for my Name, and I will establish the throne of his kingdom forever. 14 I will be his father, and he shall be my son. When he does*

wrong, I will punish him with the rod of men, with floggings inflicted by men. 15 But my love will never be taken away from him, as I took it away from Saul, whom I removed from before you. 16 Your house and your kingdom shall endure forever before me; your throne shall be established forever.'"

In 2 Samuel the Lord made a covenant with Israel's King David. The Davidic covenant promised that David would have a descendant sit on his throne forever. This covenant made it very clear that Israel's ultimate deliverer would be a man from the line of David. Within the text of the Davidic covenant, one also observes details about the punishment inflicted by men upon David's king/son.

While anyone born into the nation of Israel could be called an Israelite, it is to be understood that the spiritual Israelites are the ones who believed the promises of God. The promise of a Messiah coming from the line of David was essential to the salvation of the Israelite nation, as well as each to individual within that nation.

The New Testament, and specifically the book of Hebrews, demonstrates that Jesus is the king to sit on the throne forever. In the gospels of Matthew and Luke are found genealogies tracing the lineage of Jesus back to David through both his father (Matthew) and his mother (Luke). Jesus' lineage through his father Joseph established his legal right to the throne, while his lineage through his mother Mary demonstrated his biological relationship to David. Forty years after Jesus' death the temple was destroyed along with all the genealogical records. Jesus is the last one able to make a claim to the throne of David. Naturally, since Jesus is eternal, he will reign forever.

Jesus is the Branch of the Root of Jesse
Promised to Isaiah   (Isaiah 11:1-10)

1 ¶ A shoot will come up from the stump of Jesse; from his roots a Branch will bear fruit. 2 The Spirit of the LORD will rest on him—the Spirit of wisdom and of understanding, the Spirit of counsel and of power, the Spirit of knowledge and of the fear of the LORD— 3 and he will delight in the fear of the LORD. He will not judge by what he sees with his eyes, or decide by what he hears with his ears; 4 but with righteousness he will judge the needy, with justice he will give decisions for the poor of the earth. He will strike the earth with the rod of his mouth; with the breath of his lips he will slay the wicked. 5 Righteousness will be his belt and faithfulness the sash round his waist. 6 The wolf will live with the lamb, the leopard will lie down with the goat, the calf and the lion and the yearling together; and a little child will lead them. 7 The cow will feed with the bear, their young will lie down together, and the lion will eat straw like the ox. 8 The infant will play near the hole of the cobra, and the young child put his hand into the viper's nest. 9 They will neither harm nor destroy on all my holy mountain, for the earth will be full of the knowledge of the LORD as the waters cover the sea. 10 ¶ In that day the Root of Jesse will stand as a banner for the peoples; the nations will rally to him, and his place of rest will be glorious.

The prophet Isaiah spoke of a time when a branch of the root of Jesse will stand as a banner for the peoples. While much of Isaiah's writings are in the realm of judgment upon Israel, there are many promises for Israel's future. Jesse is the father of David. The symbolism here is that despite the waning of the nation of Israel in Isaiah's day, the root was sufficient to bear a branch.

The people of Israel would look to this branch as the one who would bring redemption to the nation and salvation to each of them. It is understood in the New Testament that Jesus is the fulfilment of the promise of a branch growing out of the root of Jesse. Paul quotes from Isaiah as he argues that Christ is a servant of the Jews on behalf of God's truth:

> And again, Isaiah says, "The Root of Jesse will spring up, one who will arise to rule over the nations; the Gentiles will hope in him." May the God of hope fill you with all joy and peace as you trust in him, so that you may overflow with hope by the power of the Holy Spirit. (Rom 15:12-13)

John, in his vision of the end of the age attributes victory to the branch:

> Then one of the elders said to me, "Do not weep! See, the Lion of the tribe of Judah, the Root of David, has triumphed. He is able to open the scroll and its seven seals." (Rev 5:5)

Jesus is the Priest to Minister Forever Promised to Jeremiah   (Jeremiah 33:14-18)

14 "'The days are coming,' declares the LORD, 'when I will fulfill the gracious promise I made to the house of Israel and to the house of Judah. 15 "'In those days and at that time I will make a righteous Branch sprout from David's line; he will do what is just and right in the land. 16 In those days Judah will be saved and Jerusalem will live in safety. This is the name by which it will be called: The LORD Our Righteousness.' 17 ¶ For this is what the LORD says: 'David will never fail to have a man to sit on the throne of the house of Israel, 18 nor will the priests, who are Levites, ever fail to have a man to stand before me continually to offer burnt offerings, to burn grain

27

offerings and to present sacrifices.'"

The prophet Jeremiah looks towards a day when the
Lord will fulfill the promises he made to Israel and Judah.
He expands on the concept of a righteous branch sprouting
from David's line to include the concept of a priest as well
as a king. Jeremiah is told by the Lord that, "David will
never fail to have a man to sit on the throne of the house of
Israel, nor will the priests, who are Levites, ever fail to have
a man stand before me continually to offer burnt offerings,
to burn grain offerings and to present sacrifices."

The one who is to come must be of the seed of
Abraham, a prophet like unto Moses, a king in the line of
David, and a priest who will stand before God forever.

The Israelites could not always anticipate how these
prophecies were to be fulfilled, but faith demanded that they
believe God would fulfill each and every prophecy. The book
of Hebrews demonstrates that Jesus fulfilled all the prophecies and especially supports his claim to the priesthood.

Jesus is the Rock to Establish a Nation
Promised to Daniel   Daniel 2:44-45)

*44 "In the time of those kings, the God of heaven will set up a
kingdom that will never be destroyed, nor will it be left to
another people. It will crush all those kingdoms and bring them
to an end, but it will itself endure forever. 45 This is the meaning of the vision of the rock cut out of a mountain, but not by
human hands—a rock that broke the iron, the bronze, the clay,
the silver and the gold to pieces. "The great God has shown the
king what will take place in the future. The dream is true and
the interpretation is trustworthy."*

The book of Daniel records prophecies made by Daniel
while he was in exile in Babylon. Included among his

prophecies is the account of a dream of Babylon's King Nebuchadnezzar as well as Daniel's subsequent interpretation. In the interpretation of the dream Daniel looked ahead to the last days. The vision of a rock destroying other kingdoms and becoming a kingdom that will endure forever refers to the kingdom of the Messiah. Once again, salvation is achieved by the one who would come rather than by a religious system or its laws. With each prophecy there is the heightened expectation that a Messianic deliverer would come.

Jesus is the Lord who will Reign
Promised to Zechariah   (Zechariah 14:4-9)

4 On that day his feet will stand on the Mount of Olives, east of Jerusalem, and the Mount of Olives will be split in two from east to west, forming a great valley, with half of the mountain moving north and half moving south. 5 You will flee by my mountain valley, for it will extend to Azel. You will flee as you fled from the earthquake in the days of Uzziah king of Judah. Then the LORD my God will come, and all the holy ones with him. 6 On that day there will be no light, no cold or frost. 7 It will be a unique day, without daytime or night-time—a day known to the LORD. When evening comes, there will be light. 8 ¶ On that day living water will flow out from Jerusalem, half to the eastern sea and half to the western sea, in summer and in winter. 9 The LORD will be king over the whole earth. On that day there will be one LORD, and his name the only name.

The prophet Zechariah looked ahead to the last days. His prophecy refers to the Messiah coming to the Mount of Olives and its splitting in two. When the Messiah comes he will establish his reign and be the king over the whole earth. Zechariah confirmed that on that day there will be one Lord and his name the only name. Zechariah made it clear that salvation will come when the Lord himself establishes his reign.

Zechariah's prophecy was undoubtedly in people's thoughts when Jesus, the Messianic candidate, arrived at the Mount of Olives for his triumphant entry into Jerusalem. On that day the Jews proclaimed him as their king but days later they rejected Jesus' Messianic candidacy and crucified him instead. If these Jews were saved by faith in a coming Messiah, what would happen if they rejected the Messiah when he arrived?

In the next chapter, examination will be made of several old covenant saints alive at the time of Christ. In each case it will be observed that they were looking for the one to come and had to make a decision whether or not Jesus was the one.

Chapter Three

Jesus is the Occasion for Writing to the Hebrews

In the previous chapter, one observes a building expectation of the coming Messiah. Beginning in the Garden of Eden the promise that God would send a redeemer intensified with each generation. Perhaps throughout history, but certainly around the time of Jesus' earthly ministry, false messiahs appeared and attracted much attention. The Jewish people were looking for the one who was to come.

Some Jews, particularly religious leaders such as the Pharisees, were content with the religion of law keeping and sacrifices. The Jews who truly understood God's plan knew that salvation had to come through an individual who would be the Messiah. In light of oppression by the Romans, the hope of the Messiah's arrival further intensified.

Into this historical background came Jesus. The question to be considered by the Jews of Jesus' day is whether he was the Messiah or not. That question was put very clearly by John the Baptist who sent his disciples to ask Jesus:

> "Are you the one who was to come, or should we expect someone else?" (Luke 7:19)

The letter to the Hebrews was written to answer the previous question. Salvation came to Old Testament saints by virtue of their faith in the coming Messiah. Hebrew people (as well as converts) who died prior to the coming of Jesus were saved and went to Paradise (Abraham's bosom) by virtue of their faith in the Messiah who would come.

When Jesus died on the cross and was resurrected, the way of salvation was forever changed and clarified. Faith was no longer in a promise, rather in the reality of the person of Jesus Christ. Those who were still alive, and saved under the old covenant trusting in a coming Messiah, were now faced with the decision to be saved under the new covenant, which is in Jesus' blood.

In essence, these saints were saved by faith in the coming Messiah but could lose that salvation if they did not believe that Jesus was the Messiah who had come. Jesus made it very clear that he was the way, the truth, and the life and that no one came to the Father except by him. (John 14:6)

No other generation of people would ever be faced with the possibility of individuals losing their salvation. This was a unique set of circumstances occurring only at the coming of Jesus.

It is a worthwhile exercise to examine many of the faithful Old Testament saints who were alive at the time of Jesus. There is Biblical evidence that each of the examples that follow moved their faith from a promised Messiah to the person of Jesus.

John the Baptist Believed Jesus was the Messiah who was to Come (Luke 7:16-23)

16 They were all filled with awe and praised God. "A great prophet has appeared among us," they said. "God has come to help his people." 17 This news about Jesus spread throughout Judea and the surrounding country. 18 John's disciples told him about all these things. Calling two of them, 19 ¶ he sent them to the Lord to ask, "Are you the one who was to come, or should we expect someone else?" 20 When the men came to Jesus, they said, "John the Baptist sent us to you to ask, 'Are you the one who was to come, or should we expect someone else?'" 21 At that very time Jesus cured many who had diseases, sicknesses and evil spirits, and gave sight to many who were blind. 22 So he replied to the messengers, "Go back and report to John what you have seen and heard: The blind receive sight, the lame walk, those who have leprosy are cured, the deaf hear, the dead are raised, and the good news is preached to the poor. 23 Blessed is the man who does not fall away on account of me."

Luke, chapter seven, records this touching account of John the Baptist upon hearing the news of Jesus' ministry. John, the forerunner of the Messiah, was in prison, and his death by beheading was just on the horizon. John was the one who pointed to Jesus and said:

"Look, the Lamb of God who takes away the sin of the world!" (John 1:29)

John was the one who baptized Jesus and heard the voice of God from heaven and saw the dove come down upon God's beloved Son. Despite these evidences of John's faith in Jesus, as the Messiah, he experienced some doubt in these last days of life. There was too much at stake not to be sure that Jesus was the true Messiah.

John sent his disciples to Jesus to ask him the question of the ages: "Are you the one who was to come or should we expect someone else?"

Jesus did not reply by saying yes I am the one. Instead he told John to examine the evidence. He told John's disciples to report to John what they had seen and heard: The blind receive sight, the lame walk, those who have leprosy are cured, the deaf hear, the dead are raised, and the good news is preached to the poor. John had been expecting and announcing that the Messiah would come. Jesus' reply is evidence that Jesus is the one.

In the twenty third verse, Jesus added another interesting insight. He said, "Blessed is the man who does not fall away on account of me." This could be understood as addressing those who were saved by trusting in a Messiah who was to come. John the Baptist certainly fit into this category. Jesus' ministry was a decision point for these individuals. They could either believe that Jesus was the Messiah and be saved by the blood he was going to shed at Calvary, or they could reject him. In the latter case they would fall away from their salvation because of their failure to receive Jesus as the Messiah who had come. Jesus would either be the rock of salvation or the stone that caused men to stumble.

Joseph Believed Jesus was the Messiah who was to Come (Matthew 1:18-25)

18 ¶ *This is how the birth of Jesus Christ came about: his mother Mary was pledged to be married to Joseph, but before they came together, she was found to be with child through the Holy Spirit. 19 Because Joseph her husband was a righteous man and did not want to expose her to public disgrace, he had in mind to divorce her quietly. 20 But after he had considered this, an angel of the Lord appeared to him in a dream and said, "Joseph son of David, do not be afraid to take Mary home as your wife, because what is conceived in her is from the Holy Spirit. 21 She will give birth to a son, and you are to give him the name Jesus, because he will save his people from their sins." 22 All this took place to fulfill what the Lord had said through the prophet: 23 "The virgin will be with child and will give birth to a son, and they will call him Emmanuel"— which means, "God with us." 24 When Joseph woke up, he did what the angel of the Lord had commanded him and took Mary home as his wife. 25 But he had no union with her until she gave birth to a son. And he gave him the name Jesus.*

34

Joseph was a devout Jew awaiting the coming of the Messiah. When the woman to whom he was betrothed became pregnant, seemingly by another man, Joseph intended to divorce her quietly. An angel visited him in a dream and told him that Mary's child was from the Holy Spirit and that the child would be the one that would save the Jewish people from their sin. The angel further instructed Joseph to marry Mary and give the son the name, Jesus. Joseph was thereby confronted with the question: Was the child, to be birthed by Mary, truly the Messiah who would save the people from their sin?

After considering the issue, Joseph obviously decided the child was the one who was to come. This is evidenced by his marriage to Mary and his obedience in naming the child Jesus. At that point he moved his faith from the promised Messiah to the Messiah, Immanuel, who had come.

The Magi Believed Jesus was the Messiah who was to Come   (Matthew 2:1-11)

1 ¶ After Jesus was born in Bethlehem in Judea, during the time of King Herod, Magi from the east came to Jerusalem 2 and asked, "'Where is the one who has been born king of the Jews? We saw his star in the east and have come to worship him." 3 When King Herod heard this he was disturbed, and all Jerusalem with him. 4 When he had called together all the people's chief priests and teachers of the law, he asked them where the Christ was to be born. 5 "In Bethlehem in Judea," they replied, "for this is what the prophet has written: 6 "'But you, Bethlehem, in the land of Judah, are by no means least among the rulers of Judah; for out of you will come a ruler who will be the shepherd of my people Israel.'" 7 Then Herod called the Magi secretly and found out from them the exact time the star had appeared. 8 He sent them to Bethlehem and said, "Go and make a careful search for the child. As soon as you find him, report to me, so that I too may go and worship him." 9 ¶ After they had heard the king, they went on their way, and the star they had seen in the east went ahead of them until it stopped over the place where the child was. 10 When they saw the star, they were overjoyed. 11 On coming to the house, they saw the child with his mother Mary, and they bowed down and worshipped him. Then they opened their treasures and presented him with gifts of gold and of incense and of myrrh.

At the time of Jesus' birth, Magi came from the East. These Magi were most likely the magicians, enchanters, diviners and wise men from the same area where Daniel had ministered some five hundred years earlier. Daniel had been put in charge of all wise men at the instructions of Nebuchadnezzar, King of Babylon. (Dan 2:48) Daniel's prophecies as recorded in his book, by the same name, showed a clear understanding of the need for an individual Messiah to save Israel. The prophecy of Daniel 9 gives a precise timetable of the events leading up to the cutting off of the Anointed One. The Anointed One is another way of saying the Messiah.

It is quite likely that the prophecies of Daniel had significant influence on the wise men who came to the birthplace of Jesus. They undoubtedly researched the timetable and combined that information with their knowledge of the star in order to make their decision to come to the land of the Jews.

There is no doubt that they were looking for the Messiah. They asked the question, "Where is the one who has been born king of the Jews?" (Matt 2:2) They were asking, "Where is the Messiah?" King Herod understood their question as evidenced by his asking the teachers of the law where the Christ was to be born. "The Christ" is the Greek language equivalent of "the Messiah." While Herod was not truly interested in worshiping the Messiah, he understood that others were looking for the Messiah's coming.

These wise men demonstrated their faith in the promise of God that a Messiah would come. They also demonstrated that they believed the baby Jesus was the Messiah. The one who was to come had come. This is clear from their bowing to worship him and giving him gifts. These wise men may even have been of Jewish ancestry. When Daniel and other members of the royal families were taken captive by Nebuchadnezzar, they were put in these high positions and became some of the greatest of the wise men of Babylon. (Dan 2:49)

Of course, whether the wise men were Jews or Gentiles does not change the fact that they were looking for the Messiah and they believed Jesus to be that Messiah.

Mary Believed Jesus was the Messiah who was to Come   (Luke 1:46-55)

46 And Mary said: "My soul glorifies the Lord 47 and my spirit rejoices in God my Savior, 48 for he has been mindful of the humble state of his servant. From now on all generations will call me blessed, 49 for the Mighty One has done great things for me—holy is his name. 50 His mercy extends to those who fear him, from generation to generation. 51 He has performed mighty deeds with his arm; he has scattered those who are proud in their inmost thoughts. 52 He has brought down rulers from their thrones but has lifted up the humble. 53 He has filled the hungry with good things but has sent the rich away empty. 54 He has helped his servant Israel, remembering to be merciful 55 to Abraham and his descendants forever, even as he said to our fathers."

When Mary was told she would give birth to a holy one called the Son of God she was also given a sign. The sign concerned the pregnancy of her cousin Elizabeth who was beyond the age of childbearing. When Mary visited Elizabeth and verified her pregnancy, Mary then broke out in song which has been called the "Magnificat."

In her song of praise, she spoke of God being her Savior. She also understood that the son within her would be the salvation of Israel. Her statement of praise demonstrated her understanding of Jesus being the fulfillment of the covenant to Abraham. She said, "He has helped his servant Israel, remembering to be merciful to Abraham and his descendants forever, even as he said to our fathers." Mary understood that the promises to her fathers, going all the way back to Abraham (and even Adam) included a seed to come. Her rejoicing over this pregnancy demonstrated that she believed Jesus was the seed of Abraham, and was the Messiah who was to come.

Simeon Believed Jesus was the Messiah who was to Come (Luke 2:25-35)

25 ¶ *Now there was a man in Jerusalem called Simeon, who was righteous and devout. He was waiting for the consolation of Israel, and the Holy Spirit was upon him. 26 It had been revealed to him by the Holy Spirit that he would not die before he had seen the Lord's Christ. 27 Moved by the Spirit, he went into the temple courts. When the parents brought in the child Jesus to do for him what the custom of the law required, 28 Simeon took him in his arms and praised God, saying: 29 "Sovereign Lord, as you have promised, you now dismiss your servant in peace. 30 For my eyes have seen your salvation, 31 which you have prepared in the sight of all people, 32 a light for revelation to the Gentiles and for glory to your people Israel." 33 The child's father and mother marveled at what was said about him. 34 Then Simeon blessed them and said to Mary, his mother: "This child is destined to cause the falling and rising of many in Israel, and to be a sign that will be*

spoken against, 35 so that the thoughts of many hearts will be revealed. And a sword will pierce your own soul too."

Forty days after the birth of Jesus, the law required Mary to be purified. Joseph and Mary took Jesus at that time to present him to the Lord in Jerusalem. While at the temple there was a wonderful encounter between Jesus and Simeon. Simeon was described as righteous and devout, one who was "waiting for the consolation of Israel." Simeon was clearly looking for the coming of the Messiah. He had the added insight revealed to him by the Holy Spirit, that he would not die before he had seen "the Lord's Christ," that is the Messiah. This righteous, devout man was saved under the old covenant by faith in the coming Messiah. When Simeon took Jesus in his arms, he looked at him and he exclaimed to God, "My eyes have seen your salvation." There was no doubt that, at that point, Simeon recognized Jesus as the Messiah who was to come. He moved his faith from the old covenant promise of a Messiah, to the new covenant reality of the person of Jesus Christ.

Simeon went on to recognize that Jesus would be the cause of the falling and rising of many in Israel. That is to say, Jesus would be the deciding factor as to the salvation or condemnation of individuals. After Jesus' resurrection, only those who believed that Jesus was the Messiah who had come would be saved. The others would fall.

Anna Believed Jesus was the Messiah who was to Come (Luke 2:36-38)

36 There was also a prophetess, Anna, the daughter of Phanuel, of the tribe of Asher. She was very old; she had lived with her husband seven years after her marriage, 37 and then was a widow until she was eighty-four. She never left the temple but worshipped night and day, fasting and praying. 38

Coming up to them at that very moment, she gave thanks to God and spoke about the child to all who were looking forward to the redemption of Jerusalem.

Following Simeon's encounter with Jesus is the account of the widow Anna. She was a prophetess who was described as one who worshiped day and night. When she saw the baby Jesus, she knew he was the Messiah. This is evidenced by her thanks to God and her testimony to others.

Anna talked about the child to "all who were looking forward to the redemption of Jerusalem." It is clear that she understood that Jesus was the Messiah and the One who would be the redemption of Jerusalem, of Israel, and of every individual who recognized him as the Messiah who had come.

The Disciples Believed Jesus was the Messiah who was to Come   (John 6:22-29; 55-71)

22 ¶ The next day the crowd that had stayed on the opposite shore of the lake realized that only one boat had been there, and that Jesus had not entered it with his disciples, but that they had gone away alone. 23 Then some boats from Tiberias landed near the place where the people had eaten the bread after the Lord had given thanks. 24 Once the crowd realized that neither Jesus nor his disciples were there, they got into the boats and went to Capernaum in search of Jesus. 25 When they found him on the other side of the lake, they asked him, "Rabbi, when did you get here?" 26 Jesus answered, "I tell you the truth, you are looking for me, not because you saw miraculous signs but because you ate the loaves and had your fill. 27 Do not work for food that spoils, but for food that endures to eternal life, which the Son of Man will give you. On him God the Father has placed his seal of approval." 28 ¶ Then they asked him, "What must we do to do the works God requires?"

29 *Jesus answered, "The work of God is this: to believe in the one he has sent."*

55 *For my flesh is real food and my blood is real drink. 56 Whoever eats my flesh and drinks my blood remains in me, and I in him. 57 Just as the living Father sent me and I live because of the Father, so the one who feeds on me will live because of me. 58 This is the bread that came down from heaven. Your forefathers ate manna and died, but he who feeds on this bread will live forever." 59 He said this while teaching in the synagogue in Capernaum.*

60 ¶ *On hearing it, many of his disciples said, "This is a hard teaching. Who can accept it?" 61 Aware that his disciples were grumbling about this, Jesus said to them, "Does this offend you? 62 What if you see the Son of Man ascend to where he was before! 63 The Spirit gives life; the flesh counts for nothing. The words I have spoken to you are spirit and they are life. 64 Yet there are some of you who do not believe." For Jesus had known from the beginning which of them did not believe and who would betray him. 65 He went on to say, "This is why I told you that no one can come to me unless the Father has enabled him."*

66 *From this time many of his disciples turned back and no longer followed him. 67 "You do not want to leave too, do you?" Jesus asked the Twelve. 68 Simon Peter answered him, "Lord, to whom shall we go? You have the words of eternal life. 69 We believe and know that you are the Holy One of God." 70 Then Jesus replied, "Have I not chosen you, the Twelve? Yet one of you is a devil!" 71 (he meant Judas, the son of Simon Iscariot, who, though one of the Twelve, was later to betray him.)*

After Jesus fed bread to the multitude, the gospel of John records an extended discourse involving Jesus, his disciples, and a crowd that followed Jesus around the lake. Jesus commented that they were looking for him, "Not because you saw miraculous signs but because you ate the loaves and had your fill." In other words they were looking for miracles for their own benefit instead of viewing them as verification that Jesus was the Messiah. They misunderstood the reason for Jesus performing miracles. As discussed previously, when John the Baptist sought confirmation that Jesus was the Messiah, Jesus offered the miracles as evidence.

Not only did the people misunderstand miracles but they misunderstood the work of God. This group asked Jesus what they must do in order to do the works that God requires. Jesus answered, "The work of God is this: to believe in the One he has sent." Jesus set aside any human achievement or successful keeping of the law in favor of simple belief that he was the Messiah who was to come.

Jesus understood that many would see him and still not believe. It was clear, however, that "on him God the Father has placed his seal of approval." (John 6:27)

During this discourse Jesus claimed to be the Bread of Life. He told the crowd that they must eat his flesh and drink his blood in order to be saved. He was moving them from the old covenant to the new covenant in his blood. At this point, many who had been following Jesus left. His attention then turned to his disciples.

Jesus asked his disciples, "You do not want to leave too, do you?" Simon Peter appointed himself spokesman for the group and answered, "Lord to whom shall we go? You have the words of eternal life. We believe and know that you are the Holy One of God." Simon Peter clearly understood that Jesus was the Holy One of God, which is another expression to say he was the Messiah. To the extent that Simon Peter's response represented all the disciples, they were no longer looking for a Messiah who was to come, but rather believed that Jesus was the Messiah who had arrived.

Peter Believed Jesus was the Messiah who was to Come (Matthew 16:13-23)

13 ¶ When Jesus came to the region of Caesarea Philippi, he asked his disciples, "Who do people say the Son of Man is?" 14 They replied, "Some say John the Baptist; others say Elijah; and still others, Jeremiah or one of the prophets." 15 "But what about you?" he asked. "Who do you say I am?" 16 Simon Peter answered, "You are the Christ, the Son of the living God." 17 Jesus replied, "Blessed are you, Simon son of Jonah, for this was not revealed to you by man, but by my Father in heaven. 18 And I tell you that you are Peter, and on this rock I will build my church, and the gates of Hades will not overcome it. 19 I will give you the keys of the kingdom of heaven; whatever you bind on earth will be bound in heaven, and whatever you loose on earth will be loosed in heaven." 20 Then he warned his disciples not to tell anyone that he was the Christ. 21 ¶ From that time on Jesus began to explain to his disciples that he must go to Jerusalem and suffer many things at the hands of the elders, chief priests and teachers of the law, and that he must be killed and on the third day be raised to life. 22 Peter took him aside and began to rebuke him. "Never, Lord!" he said. "This shall never happen to you!" 23 Jesus turned and said to Peter, "Get behind me, Satan! You are a stumbling-block to me; you do not have in mind the things of God, but the things of men."

Simon Peter's confession of Jesus as the Messiah could not have been clearer than when Jesus and his disciples were at Caesarea Philippi. Jesus asked his disciples: "Who do people say that I am?" Simon Peter replied, "You are the Christ, the Son of the Living God." Once again, the expression "the Christ" is the Greek equivalent of the Messiah. Peter moved his faith from a Messiah who was to come, to

Jesus Christ, the Messiah who had arrived.

In the exchange that followed, between Jesus and Peter, it was apparent that Peter did not understand the entire plan. He objected to Jesus' going to Jerusalem and suffering and dying. He said, "Never Lord! This shall never happen to you!" Jesus rebuked Peter for his statement and said, "Get behind me Satan! You are a stumbling block to me." Jesus knew that the mere coming of the Messiah was insufficient for the redemption of man. The Messiah also had to suffer, die, and be raised from the dead on the third day. True salvation comes when one believes Jesus is the Christ but also believes that he went to the cross and died for the sin of mankind. Peter would certainly evidence this kind of faith after the resurrection.

Conclusion Concerning Whether Jesus Was the Messiah who was to Come

In each of the examples above, there was a devout Jew or convert who was looking for the coming of the Messiah and the redemption of Israel. As each had an encounter with Jesus, each in turn had an opportunity to evaluate whether Jesus was the Messiah who had come. Accepting that fact brought them salvation, while rejecting Jesus as the Messiah, who had come, caused them to fall away, regardless of their previous faith. Major issues have to be addressed. Assume that someone was saved under the old covenant by faith in the coming Messiah. If he died prior to Jesus' arrival, he would have been in Paradise. Once Jesus came, died, and was resurrected, Jesus was the only way of salvation. If that same Old Testament saint, who was saved by faith in the coming Messiah, rejected Jesus as being the Messiah, was he still saved? Does salvation in the Old Testament include the aspects of eternal security that

Christians enjoy today? What happened to Old Testament saints, living outside Jerusalem, who died after the resurrection but had not heard about Jesus?

The years just after Jesus' resurrection were a unique time in Biblical history. The outworkings of the old covenant, including its temple worship, continued until 70 AD. Meanwhile, the new covenant in Christ's blood began operation in approximately 30 AD. That forty year generation was ushering out the old and obsolete while ushering in the new. They were leaving the shadow and entering the reality. It was to this unique generation that Hebrews was written. Its purpose was to inform the Hebrews, who were looking for the Messiah, that he had come and to persuade them to believe that Jesus of Nazareth was indeed the Messiah who had come.

With this understanding of the purpose of the book of Hebrews, many of the difficult passages fall into place and are quite understandable. While this author does not believe a Christian can lose his salvation, there is no such assurance given to the one saved under the old covenant who rejected Jesus as being the one who fulfilled that covenant.

Chapter Four

Jesus is a Message Superior to Any Other   (1:1 to 1:3)

He is a Better Method of Communication than that of the Past   (1:1-2)

1 ¶ In the past God spoke to our forefathers through the prophets at many times and in various ways, 2 but in these last days he has spoken to us by his Son, whom he appointed heir of all things, and through whom he made the universe.

Mankind has a desire for God in his heart but no way to find him. The only way God can be revealed to mankind is if God initiates it himself. Over time, God has chosen to reveal himself with ever increasing effectiveness. Eventually, his revelation of himself came in bodily form. Nothing is a clearer revelation of God than Jesus. The book of Hebrews begins by making it clear that Jesus is the ultimate communication from God.

The Written Word of the Prophets

1 ¶ In the past God spoke to our forefathers through the prophets at many times and in various ways,

Hebrews begins with a summary of God's work in the past. It is no small thing to say that God spoke. He is the creator of all things, he did not have to speak. On the contrary, given man's propensity to sin, as evidenced in the

Garden of Eden, God could have simply wiped mankind off the face of the earth. Instead, he chose to reveal his will and his plan to mankind.

God chose to speak to the forefathers of the Hebrews. His communications to mankind were meticulously preserved by the Hebrew nation. Scripture became the permanent record of the communications from God. The first Scriptures were written by the very hand of God on Mount Sinai. After God wrote the Ten Commandments, Moses, under the inspiration of the Holy Spirit, recorded the remainder of the law.

God spoke through the prophets. These men, who included former prophets such as Moses, Joshua, and Samuel, were God's chosen instruments of communication. The Apostle Peter reminds us:

> Above all, you must understand that no prophecy of Scripture came about by the prophet's own interpretation. For prophecy never had its origin in the will of man, but men spoke from God as they were carried along by the Holy Spirit. (2 Peter 1:20-21)

God could have written the entire Bible and dropped it from the sky. He chose, however, to use ordinary men to record and preserve his Word for all generations.

God spoke at many times. The Greek word translated "at many times" is the word "polumeros" which means "many portions." The King James translation is "divers manners." The root of the word comes from the prefix poly meaning many. Current usage of this word includes "polygamist" who is one with many wives and "polytheist" who is one with many gods. The idea is that God did not give his revelation in one piece but rather in many portions.

At a recent church event there was an occasion for serving a large sheet cake. The cake was decorated with a congratulatory message to a couple who had just adopted twins from Vietnam. The cake was served in various portions. Some individuals asked for very large portions because they enjoyed chocolate cake. Others received simply regular sized portions. Still others asked for just a sliver of cake because they were watching their weight. The cake was served in various portions. While each portion of the cake had a piece of the overall message, the message could not be discerned unless all the pieces were viewed together. This is illustrative of how God served his message to the prophets.

God in his sovereignty may have served a large portion to Moses or Samuel or Isaiah, while giving a small portion to Obadiah or Habakkuk. These prophets were given their portions over a fifteen- hundred-year period prior to the coming of Christ. Each portion was part of God's unfolding revelation of himself.

God's revelation has been given to mankind in a progressive manner. Moses' record of the Garden of Eden recorded the beginning revelation of God. At the time of the fall of man due to the sin of Adam and Eve, God gave a prophecy that a male seed of the woman would crush Satan's head. This initial promise of a coming Messiah was expanded upon throughout the years until eventually that promised Messiah came.

God spoke in various ways. Not only did God speak to many prophets, with many portions, but he also did it in many ways. The prophets record that God spoke through direct speech, angels, visions, animals, signs, wonders, circumstances of life, etc. In each situation, God chose the best method of communication for the portion of his revelation being communicated at that time.

The Living Word - Jesus

2 but in these last days he has spoken to us by his Son, whom he appointed heir of all things, and through whom he made the universe.

Think again about the illustration of a cake being served in many portions. The original congratulatory message on the cake became more difficult to discern as the cake was served. Each person took his slice to a different location and the completed cake was never seen again. Fortunately someone had taken a picture of the cake before it was divided into portions and the entire message of the cake was preserved.

In God's revelation of his will, each portion was given out and the totality of the message was unclear to the prophets. Fortunately, God had another method of revealing himself to mankind. This method was his Son. His Son was not simply another portion of the message but rather Jesus was the whole cake.

The Son came in these last days. There is a tendency of some to understand this as an eschatological reference. Inasmuch as two thousand years have passed since the Son came, it seems unlikely that this passage refers to the end of days. It is preferable to see this as the last days of Biblical revelation. With the coming of the Son and the completion of the New Testament account of that coming, the revelation of God reached its last days. There was no need for God to say anything else after he sent his Son.

God has spoken to us by his Son. The actual Greek text says that God has spoken to us "in Son". In other words Jesus was not the messenger but the message. He was not the method of communication but the communication itself. He did not come to tell us about God but to be God with us. Jesus is not the last piece of the cake completing God's revelation. He is rather the totality of the revelation. All of the portions provided in the Old Testament were types and shadows of something to come. Jesus is not a type or shadow but rather the antitype and reality. This is why Jesus said in Matthew 5:17:

> "Do not think that I have come to abolish the law or the prophets; I have not come to abolish them but to fulfill them."

Jesus is the fulfillment of the entire Old Testament.

In the verses that follow, the writer to the Hebrews describes who the Son is by viewing some of his attributes and activities. Throughout the remainder of the book of Hebrews, the author will show that Jesus is superior to anything in the past. This includes angels, Moses, priests, etc. The purpose was to move people from faith in a coming Messiah, revealed in types and shadows, to faith in the Messiah who had come, revealed in the reality of Jesus the Son.

Jesus is the heir of all things. Generally, one thinks of an heir as the person who would inherit the family estate upon the death of the father. Obviously, this definition cannot be in view when dealing with an eternal God that will never cease to live. An insight into how the concept of being an heir applies to Jesus can be derived from Psalm 2. This is a Messianic Psalm well known to the Hebrews. The writer to the Hebrews quotes from this Psalm seven times. One such quote is from verse seven: "You are my Son; today I have become your Father." This particular quote can be found in Hebrews 1:5 and 5:5. As will be expounded later, the fulfillment of this Messianic prophecy comes at the resurrection of Jesus.

Inasmuch as an heir's inheritance involves death it is fitting that Christ's inheritance is tied into his defeating of death through his resurrection. The verse that follows in Psalm 2 says:

> Ask of me, and I will make the nations your

inheritance, the ends of the earth your possession. You will rule them with an iron scepter; you will dash them to pieces like pottery.

This is a description of the inheritance of the resurrected Son. All nations and all possessions on the earth will be his and he will be the sovereign ruler of all there is.

It is encouraging to be reminded that Christians are described as sons as well as co-heirs with Christ. Jesus is the sole heir; however, those who have received him as their Savior have been incorporated into the only begotten Son (Romans 8:14-17; Galatians 4:4-7; 1 Peter 1:3-5). Mankind could never be heirs of God in their own right, but by sharing in the divine nature (2 Pet 1:4) and the righteousness of Christ (2 Cor 5:21), they can become joint heirs with him.

The Son is the One through whom God made the universe. Jesus was present and participated in the creation of the world. Genesis 1:26 reveals a multiple presence at creation when God said "Let us make men in our image, in our likeness..." This multiple presence is understood to be God the Father, God the Son, and God the Holy Spirit.

The Apostle Paul gives further insight into Jesus' role at creation. In writing to the church at Colosse Paul states in chapter one, verse 15 and 16:

> He (Jesus) is the image of the invisible God, the firstborn over all creation. For by him all things were created: things in heaven and on earth, visible and invisible, whether thrones or powers or rulers or authorities; all things were created by him and for him.

The Son has always coexisted with the Father. The early church father, Athanasius explains that: "When the sacred writers say that he is before all ages and that through him he created the world, they proclaim the eternal and everlasting being of the Son and thereby designate him as God." The Hebrews understood "Son of God" to include the concept of him as being one with God and equal to God in every way. References to Jesus creating the world demonstrate his divine nature.

He is the Representation of God to Mankind (1:3)

3 The Son is the radiance of God's glory and the exact representation of his being, sustaining all things by his powerful word. After he had provided purification for sins, he sat down at the right hand of the Majesty in heaven.

Mankind craves knowing God in an intimate and personal way. Apart from Jesus this is not possible. Jesus is called Immanuel, which means, "God with us." He is the chosen method of communication between God and Man and is the exact representation of God. Anyone who has seen Jesus has seen the Father. The author of Hebrews establishes the nature and work of the Son in these early verses positioning them as an overview of his entire argument for the book. He will continue throughout his letter to demonstrate the superiority of Jesus to all things.

The Radiance of God's Glory

3a The Son is the radiance of God's glory and the exact representation of his being, sustaining all things by his powerful word.

The Son is the radiance of God's glory. Jesus is the exact representation of God's glory. He is not simply a reflection of it. Jesus is the radiance of God in the way that light is the radiance of the sun.

During a church service on a bright Sunday morning I commented, "Isn't it nice to have the sun coming in the window?" Everyone understood what I meant. But, an analysis of that statement could create a ludicrous picture of a ball of fire traveling ninety three million miles to enter the sanctuary window. While that sphere did not make the trip, the light from it did. It was no less a representation of the sun than if we had traveled to its surface. If man were to look directly at the sun his eyes would be blinded. It is interesting, however, that without the rays of light from that sun, man would also be unable to see. Similarly, man cannot look at God and live. Yet, without looking to God's exact representation, man also cannot live.

Jesus is the exact representation of his being. The Nicene Creed describes Jesus as "being of one substance with the Father." This is what is being expressed by the term "exact representation." Jesus is God and God is Jesus; if one has seen Jesus one has seen God.

This was made clear by Jesus himself in the upper room discourse. The Apostle Philip requested, "Lord show us the Father and that will be enough for us" (John 14:8). Jesus' response to Philip was:

> "Don't you know Me, Philip, even after I have been among you such a long time? Anyone who has seen me has seen the Father. How can you say, show us the Father?" (John 14:9)

In this mild rebuke of Philip, Jesus made it clear that there is nothing more to see. He is the exact representation of God's being.

Jesus sustains all things by his powerful word. In the

beginning the world was spoken into existence. God simply said, "Let there be light, and it was so." In Hebrews is a reminder that Jesus continues to sustain this world by his word. Again, referring to the Apostle Paul's letter to the Colossians, chapter 1:17 says of Jesus, "He is before all things and in him all things hold together." The universe is held in a delicate balance. God did not simply create the universe and then let it run by itself. This is the false view of the Deist. In reality, God the Son must stay continually involved to keep the universe in sync. Jesus' involvement as the sustainer of all things includes the physical universe as well as the spiritual, and all other aspects of life. Jesus is the cosmic glue that holds everything together.

The Redemption of God's Creation

3b After he had provided purification for sins, he sat down at the right hand of the Majesty in heaven.

Jesus provided purification for sins. As part of his sustaining of the universe, Jesus had to deal with an assault upon that created universe. Mankind, the high point of God's creation, had fallen into sin and was condemned to eternal death (Romans 3:23). Inasmuch as mankind was made to worship God forever, the sin problem had to be dealt with. The reason for its needing to be resolved went beyond being a benefit to mankind. It needed to be done in order for God's plan for the universe to reach its fruition.

Inasmuch as the wages of mankind's sin was death, a substitute to die on man's behalf was needed. Jesus was that substitute. When he went to the cross of Calvary and died, he provided purification for the sins that man had committed. Through faith in Jesus, man could be made right with God and order in the universe be restored.

Jesus sat down at the right hand of the Majesty in

heaven. The expression that Jesus sat down implies that his work of purification was finished. The concept of sitting does not imply inactivity. It is rather a clear statement that nothing more needed to be done to provide for the purification of man's sins. This will be expanded later in the book when the ceaseless activities of the priests in the earthly temple are contrasted with the "once-for-all" completed activity of Jesus.

Jesus is not only seated but he is seated "at the right hand of the Majesty on High." This expression expresses the power that has been given to Jesus. The right hand is the place of power and authority. Jesus has been elevated to the highest place. He is the King of Kings and Lord of Lords, at whose name every knee shall bow and every tongue confess that Jesus Christ is Lord. (Philippians 2:11)

It is important to note that Jesus' completion of the work of purification leaves nothing for man to do. Luther put it this way:

> "Therefore we must despair of our own penances and our own purging of our sins, because before we even begin to confess, our sins have already been forgiven. I would even go on to say, that it is not till then (i.e., until we despair of own penance and purging), that Christ's own purging becomes operative, and produces true repentance in us." (Hughes p 59)

These initial verses of Hebrews have set the stage. Jesus has been presented as the ultimate communication to mankind. All the promises, the law and the prophecies have found their fulfillment in the person of Jesus. Throughout the history of the Hebrews, the message was that a Messiah would come to save the people. Spiritual Jews believed in the promise of the coming Messiah and were saved. The writer to the Hebrews has made the claim that Jesus is the One who was to come. The remainder of the book of Hebrews supports this thesis and makes it clear that Jesus is the one who was to come.

Chapter Five

Jesus is a Mediator
Superior to Angels   (1:4 to 2:9)

He has a Better Inherited Name
than the Angels   (1:4-5)

4 ¶ So he became as much superior to the angels as the name he has inherited is superior to theirs. 5 For to which of the angels did God ever say, "You are my Son; today I have become your Father"? Or again, "I will be his Father, and he will be my Son"?

Having previously concluded that the Son is a superior method of communication than everything that came through the prophets, the author moves his argument to the next phase. Remember that the author is attempting to persuade the Hebrews that Jesus is the one who was to come, the Messiah. Throughout his section on angels, which ends at chapter two, verse nine, the writer will demonstrate the superiority of the Son over angels. The name Jesus is not mentioned until the final verse of the section.

The author carefully constructs his argument from Old Testament Messianic texts in such a way that the Hebrews would have to agree with him. Only after agreement as to the nature of the Son does he point to Jesus as the one. It is a masterful argument that leads them to the inescapable conclusion that Jesus, the Son of God, is the one who was to come.

Angels held an important role in Jewish history. Although Old Testament accounts did not give all the details, there are two New Testament texts that discuss the angels' role as ordaining the covenant and being mediators at the giving of the law. Paul writes the following to the Galatians:

> What, then, was the purpose of the law? It was added because of transgressions until the Seed to whom the promise referred had come. The law was put into effect through angels by a mediator. (Gal 3:19)

In Acts, chapter seven, Luke records for us the words of Stephen:

> "...you who have received the law that was put into effect through angels but have not obeyed it." (Acts 7:53)

These created beings were held in high regard by the Hebrews. They were considered the most excellent of all creatures. The writer to the Hebrews will demonstrate that there is one who is more excellent and whose inherited name is superior to the angels.

He has Become Superior to Angels

4 ¶ So he became as much superior to the angels as the name he has inherited is superior to theirs.

The term "he became" is better translated as a participial phrase, "having become." In either case, there seems to be a point in time when something occurred. This has to be reconciled with Christian orthodox understanding that Jesus is eternally existing with the Father. There was never a time when the second person of the Trinity did not exist. There are at least four suggested events at which Jesus inherited the name Son. The first is at the incarnation recorded in the book of Luke:

> He will be great and will be called the Son of the Most High. The Lord God will give him the throne of his father David, (Luke 1:32)

Some would suggest that the term "Son" deals with Jesus after his incarnation. John MacArthur concludes:

> The Bible nowhere speaks of the eternal Sonship of Christ. When his eternity is spoken of in Hebrews 1:8, God says to the Son, "Thy throne, O God, is forever and ever." When talking about Christ's eternity, the title "God" is used; only when talking about his incarnation is he called "Son." (MacArthur, p 27)

The second significant event at which the designation "Son" is used for Jesus is at his baptism as recorded in Mark:

> And a voice came from heaven: "You are my Son, whom I love; with you I am well pleased." (Mark 1:11)

The designation is also used at the transfiguration of Jesus in Luke:

> A voice came from the cloud, saying, "This is my Son, whom I have chosen; listen to him." (Luke 9:35)

In Romans, the Apostle Paul cites the resurrection as the point at which Jesus was declared the Son:

> regarding his Son, who as to his human nature was a descendant of David, and who through the Spirit of holiness was declared with power to be the Son of God, by his resurrection from the dead: Jesus Christ our Lord. (Rom 1:3-4)

Philip Hughes quotes Augustine's conclusion to the issue:

> Christ according to his humanity who, while he was mortal, was the Son of man, clothed himself in the resurrection with immortality and became the Son of God, in such a way, however, that he did not cease to be the Son of man, because he remained true man. (Hughes, 55)

In this way Augustine recognizes Jesus' designation as Son of man at his first birth while giving him the designation Son of God at his second birth, the resurrection from the dead. In neither case does he imply that Jesus was ever anything less than coequal with God.

The issue of when Jesus received the designation "Son" is clarified by the verse that follows in the text of Hebrews.

He is the Unique Son of the Father

5 For to which of the angels did God ever say, "You are my Son; today I have become your Father"? Or again, "I will be his Father, and he will be my Son"?

This quotation is from Psalm 2:7. This particular Psalm is clearly understood by the Hebrews as a Messianic Psalm. The question to be considered is, "When does that Messianic prophecy find its fulfillment?" The answer is found in the book of Acts which records a message given at Pisidian Antioch by the Apostle Paul:

> We tell you the good news: What God promised our fathers he has fulfilled for us, their children, by raising up Jesus. As it is written in the second Psalm, "You are my Son; today I have become your Father." (Acts 13:32-33)

Paul makes it abundantly clear that the prophecy of Psalm 2:7 is fulfilled when Jesus Christ is raised. Jesus, who has been eternally equal to the Father, is declared the Son at His resurrection.

Jesus is the only individual declared to be the Son of God. There are instances in Genesis 6:2 and Job 38:7 where angels, in their totality, are referred to as sons of God. This designation deals with the fact that God created all the angels and that, in some way, they reflect him. There is never, however, an instance where an individual angel is singled out for the designation "son."

It is a rhetorical question that the writer to the Hebrews poses when he asks: "For to which of the angels did God ever say..." The answer is obvious to the Hebrews that God never said that to any of the angels.

The writer next quotes from 2 Samuel 7:

> "I will be his Father and he will be My Son." (2 Sam 7:14)

This is taken from the Davidic covenant. The prophet

Nathan, speaking to David, promised that there will be an offspring to succeed him and that his throne will be established forever. The short-term fulfillment of this could be seen in the birth of David's son Solomon who would sit on the throne. It is obvious, however, that someone to sit on the throne for eternity would have to be eternal, so this speaks of a future king, the Messiah. The reference quoted in Hebrews is from verse 14 of 2 Samuel 7. The remainder of that verse says:

> "When he does wrong I will punish him with the rod of men, with floggings inflicted by men."

It is obvious that the punishment of the Messiah is in view in this text. This finds its fulfillment at the death of Christ when he takes upon himself the wrongs of mankind and is punished for them. This fits extremely well with the conclusion that the declaration as Son came at Jesus' resurrection.

Obviously, the tense of this quote from the Davidic covenant is future. By using the construction "I will be," it implies something will be new in the relationship between the members of the Godhead. It in no way implies that Jesus is anything less than eternal and coequal with God. However, in the events of his incarnation, and ultimately at his resurrection, he receives a new designation and a new title as Son.

He Holds a Better Position in Eternity Future   (1:6-9)

6 *And again, when God brings his firstborn into the world, he says, "Let all God's angels worship him." 7 In speaking of the angels he says, "He makes his angels winds, his servants flames of fire." 8 But about the Son he says, "Your throne, O God, will last*

forever and ever, and righteousness will be the sceptre of your kingdom. 9 You have loved righteousness and hated wickedness; therefore God, your God, has set you above your companions by anointing you with the oil of joy."

In continuing to argue for the supremacy of the Son over angels, the author of Hebrews turns to the future. Continuing to quote from the Old Testament, he seeks to gain the Hebrews' assent to the fact that the Son is greater than angels.

A question to be answered is whether the word "again" goes with the verb "says" or with the verb "brings." If the author is saying, "he says again" then it simply introduces a new quotation. On the other hand, if the author is saying, "when he brings again" then it is speaking of the second coming of the Son into the world. The Greek word order is "and whenever again he brings in the firstborn into the world, he says." This would connect the term "again" with the bringing as opposed to the saying. It is apparent that this is a reference to the Son being brought into the world again. It speaks of the second coming of Jesus Christ. The author describes the relationship between angels and the Son, particularly in relation to his return to the earth.

He will be Worshipped by Angels

6 And again, when God brings his firstborn into the world, he says, "Let all God's angels worship him."

Jesus' designation as firstborn is used frequently in the New Testament. In addition to uses involving Jesus' incarnation, he is referred to as the firstborn from the dead in Colossians 1:18 and Revelation 1:5. This is similar to 1 Corinthians 15:20 where Paul calls Jesus, "the firstfruits of those who have fallen asleep." It is likely that the writer has this view of firstborn in mind as he writes. This is particularly so, since the conclusion of his argument for this section of the book comes in chapter two, verse nine:

> But we see Jesus who was made a little lower than the angels now crowned with glory and honor because he suffered death, so that by the grace of God he might taste death for everyone.

Inasmuch as the writer points to Jesus' claim of superiority as being related to his death, it is likely that his reference to firstborn deals with his resurrection from the dead as opposed to his incarnation.

This also seems to fit the context of his Old Testament reference:

> "Let all God's angels worship him."

This is a reference to Psalm 97 which refers to the second coming:

> The LORD reigns, let the earth be glad; let the distant shores rejoice. Clouds and thick darkness surround him; righteousness and justice are the foundation of his throne. Fire goes before him and consumes his foes on every side. His lightning lights up the world; the earth sees and trembles. The mountains melt like wax before the LORD, before the Lord of all the earth. The heavens proclaim his righteousness, and all the peoples see his glory. All who worship images are put to shame, those who boast in idols—worship him, all you gods! (Psalm 97:1-7)

ᒼᵖ˙

Jesus is a Mediator Superior to Angels

The Massoretic Hebrew text says "sons of God" (this is translated "all you gods" in the NIV). The author of Hebrews, however, takes all of his Old Testament quotations from the Septuagint, which clearly states, "All you his angels, worship him."

It is not to be concluded that angels do not worship the Son until his second coming. It is clear that they have worshiped at his birth, and currently worship around his throne (Rev 5:11-12). The point, however, is that he will return and receive the worship of the angels, demonstrating his clear superiority to them.

He is Served by Angels

7 In speaking of the angels he says, "He makes his angels winds, his servants flames of fire."

Again, utilizing the Old Testament as his authority, the writer quotes Psalm 104:4. In applying this Psalm to the Son, he continues to demonstrate the Son's superiority to the angels. The angels are referred to as "his angels;" this indicates that they belong to the Son. They are also referred to as his servants. This is a clear indication of their inferiority to the Son.

In addition, the word used for "he makes" is the Greek word "poieo" which means "to create." This could imply the fact that the Son created the angels (Colossians 1:16).

The suggestion that angels are made winds and flames could have a number of meanings. Winds could also be translated spirits, which is certainly indicative of the nature of angels. Likewise, flames of fire could be a reference to particular angels called seraphim which is a Hebrew term meaning "burning ones."

Winds and flames could also refer to angels being changed into those things that God wants to use at a particular time. Perhaps the wind and fire at Pentecost were a manifestation of angelic beings.

Lastly, it is possible that the reference to winds and flames is simply to demonstrate that angels are created beings to do God's will as are other elements of nature. In any case, the point is that the Son is superior to these, his servants.

He Will Rule Forever

8 But about the Son he says, "Your throne, O God, will last forever and ever, and righteousness will be the sceptre of your kingdom.

The author now indicates that the Son will sit on a throne. No angel has ever been enthroned. The one recorded attempt of an angel to sit enthroned is in Isaiah 14 and involves the fall of the angel Lucifer from heaven. One who sits on a throne is superior to those who serve.

The quotation is taken from Psalm 45, verse 8. It is a Psalm that describes the nature of the Messiah with an emphasis on his kingship. The quoted verse speaks of the duration of the Messiah's throne which is for all eternity. It also refers to the Messiah as God. There are a number of Old Testament prophecies that address the Messiah as God. In Isaiah 9:6 he is referred to as the "Mighty God." Jeremiah called him "Yahweh Tsidkenu," which means Jehovah our righteousness. This is a clear reference to the Messiah being Yahweh, the covenant name for God.

The fact that God is mankind's righteousness is picked up in this quote, from Psalm 45, that says righteousness will be the scepter of your kingdom. The rule of the Messiah will be marked by absolute justice.

This particular text, when applied to Jesus, becomes the clearest statement of his deity in all of Scripture. There is no doubt that the Son is referred to as God.

He has been Set Above his Companions

9 You have loved righteousness and hated wickedness; therefore God, your God, has set you above your companions by anointing you with the oil of joy."

The author continues to quote from Psalm 45. The Psalm is not describing the eternal holiness of the Son, rather describing his role as the one who was to come, that is, the Messiah. The Messiah would be characterized as one who loved righteousness and hated wickedness.

As a result of the Messiah's character and activities, he would be set above his companions. This could simply be a reference to angels or it could be a reference to mankind. In either case the importance of the statement is that the Messiah is greater than all others.

The oil of joy is likely a reference to his beginning to reign in the Messianic Age. Typically, kings were anointed with oil to designate their appointment as king. Saul and David, the first kings of Israel were so anointed. The very nature of the Hebrew word "Messiah" implies "the anointed one."

Again, there is a strong reference to the Son being God. Addressing the Son, the psalmist says, "Therefore God, your God has set you above your companions." In this direct address the Son is called God. Applying this to Jesus again eliminates all question about his deity.

He holds a Better Position in Eternity Past   (1:10-12)

10 He also says, "In the beginning, O Lord, you laid the foundations of the earth, and the heavens are the work of your hands. 11 They will perish, but you remain; they will all wear out like a garment. 12 You will roll them up like a robe; like a garment they will be changed. But you remain the same, and your years will never end."

Having demonstrated the Son is superior in eternity future, the author of Hebrews now turns his attention to eternity past. Once again he demonstrates that Jesus, the Son, has always been superior to the angels.

He Created the Universe

10 He also says, "In the beginning, O Lord, you laid the foundations of the earth, and the heavens are the work of your hands..."

The writer again appeals to the Psalm as his authority for the superiority of the Son. He attributes Psalm 102, verses 25 through 27, to the Son. He gives to him the credit for creating the entire universe. This is consistent with Paul's teaching in Colossians, chapter one:

> For by him all things were created: things in heaven and on earth, visible and invisible, whether thrones or powers or rulers or authorities; all things were created by him and for him. (Col 1:16)

Obviously, the creator is superior to the creation, of which the angels are a part.

He will Endure Beyond the Universe

11 "... They will perish, but you remain; they will all wear out like a garment. 12 You will roll them up like a robe; like a garment they will be changed. But you remain the same, and your years will never end."

While viewing the Son as creator, the author also demonstrates that he endures beyond the creation. The creation will perish like a garment but Jesus will remain. There are a number of New Testament references that can support this concept. While the quote from Psalm 102 refers to rolling the creation up like a robe, the book of Revelation speaks in a similar manner of a scroll:

> The sky receded like a scroll, rolling up, and every mountain and island was removed from its place. (Rev 6:14)

The idea of taking off a garment and changing to a new one refers to the creation of a new universe as described in 2 Peter:

> Since everything will be destroyed in this way, what kind of people ought you to be? You ought to live holy and godly lives as you look forward to the day of God and speed its coming. That day will bring about the destruction of the heavens by fire, and the elements will melt in the heat. But in keeping with his promise we are looking forward to a new heaven and a new earth, the home of righteousness. (2 Peter 3:12-13)

The conjunction "but" presents a strong contrast between the perishability of the created universe and the durability of the Son. He will remain the same and his years will never end. This affirmation is reiterated in Hebrews 13:

Jesus Christ is the same yesterday and today
and forever. (Heb 13:8)

Just as the Creator is superior to the creation, the One
that endures beyond the creation is superior to that which
comes to an end.

He has a Better Location
for Current Ministry   (1:13-14)

*13 To which of the angels did God ever say, "Sit at my right
hand until I make your enemies a footstool for your feet?" 14
Are not all angels ministering spirits sent to serve those who
will inherit salvation?*

The writer of Hebrews has looked to the future to
demonstrate the superiority of the Son over angels, he has
looked to the past to make the same point, and he now looks
at the present position of both the Son and the angels.

He is Seated at God's Right Hand

*13 To which of the angels did God ever say, "Sit at my right
hand until I make your enemies a footstool for your feet?"*

The writer appeals to Psalm 110 to demonstrate that the
Son is now seated at the right hand of God. The Psalm
begins, "the Lord says to my Lord." This is similar in wording to Psalm 45 which says "therefore God, your God has
set you above your companions." In Psalm 45 both the
Father and the Son are referred to as God. In Psalm 110 both
the Father and the Son are referred to as Lord. The first
reference to Lord speaks of the Father and is the translation
of the Hebrew "Yahweh." The second use of Lord speaks to
the Son and is a translation of the Hebrew "Adonai." In both

cases these are divine names.

Jesus used this Psalm to confound the Pharisees. The record of that encounter is found in Matthew, chapter 22:

> While the Pharisees were gathered together, Jesus asked them, "What do you think about the Christ? Whose son is he?" "The son of David," they replied. He said to them, "How is it then that David, speaking by the Spirit, calls him 'Lord?' For he says, "'The Lord said to my Lord: "Sit at my right hand until I put your enemies under your feet.'" If then David calls him 'Lord', how can he be his son?" No one could say a word in reply, and from that day on no one dared to ask him any more questions.

Jesus was using Psalm 110 to demonstrate the superiority of the Son even to King David. The Messiah would be more than the son of David, he would be David's Lord and God.

While Jesus used this Psalm to demonstrate superiority to David, the writer to Hebrews used it to demonstrate superiority to angels. The rhetorical question was asked, "To which of the angels did God ever say, 'Sit at my right hand until I make your enemies a footstool for your feet?'" The answer is, to none of them. It was only to the Messiah that this invitation was made.

Obviously, this quotation does not mean that the Messiah's reign will end when all enemies have been brought under his feet. It has already been established previously that his throne is forever and ever. This simply means that even though there are still enemies to be put in subjection to the Messiah, he is nonetheless reigning even now. His current position at the right hand of God is superior to that of the angels.

He Sends Forth Angels

14 Are not all angels ministering spirits sent to serve those who will inherit salvation?

In contrast to the exalted position of the Son, the angels are ministering spirits serving mankind. Angels are spirits, characterized by being invisible and swift in service.

They are sent to serve. Obviously the one who sends them is God or even perhaps the Son. Their service is in the realm of ministering to those who will inherit salvation.

While it is difficult to know all the ways angels serve mankind there are glimpses in Scripture. For instance, in 2 Kings 6:15, Elisha's servant was permitted to see a mountain full of horses and chariots of fire around Elisha.

Angels ministered to the shepherds at the birth of Christ (Luke 2:13) and angels announced the resurrection of Jesus. (Luke 24:4)

The fact that angels minister in this way is not demeaning but rather glorious. Nonetheless, their ministry is far inferior to the ministry of the Son who is seated on the throne.

He Announces a Better Message than the Law   (2:1-4)

1 ¶ We must pay more careful attention, therefore, to what we have heard, so that we do not drift away. 2 For if the message spoken by angels was binding, and every violation and disobedience received its just punishment, 3 how shall we escape if we ignore such a great salvation? This salvation, which was first announced by the Lord, was confirmed to us by those who heard him. 4 God also testified to it by signs, wonders and various miracles, and gifts of the Holy Spirit distributed according to his will.

In his first chapter, the author of Hebrews made a compelling argument that Jesus is superior to the angels. The purpose of his writing was not just to communicate information but to bring his readers to a point of decision. Remember, he was writing to devout Jews who were saved by their faith in the promise that a Messiah would come. The author wanted to demonstrate that Jesus was the Messiah who has come and to urge them to put their faith in him.

The second chapter of Hebrews begins an invitation, which concludes at verse nine, where Jesus is offered as the one who has tasted death for everyone.

The transitional word "therefore" in the text demonstrates that the author was drawing a conclusion from everything that was said in chapter one. Based on everything he has said thus far, he encouraged the Hebrews to make a decision.

His Message Deserves more Careful Attention

1 ¶ We must pay more careful attention, therefore, to what we have heard, so that we do not drift away.

The author begins with the word "we" thereby including himself among the group of devout Jews to which he is writing. The author is undoubtedly a Hebrew. Perhaps he is a Hebrew of Hebrews, such as Paul, who describes himself in such a manner. (Phil 3:5)

The desire of the writer is that they pay more careful attention to what they have heard. The Greek word so translated is "prosecho". It is used in Hebrews 7:13 in speaking of the priests who "served" at the altar. In both cases a literal translation could be rendered "to be devoted to."

Understanding of the nature of the priesthood would give insight into the meticulous service by the priest. He would of necessity be carefully devoted to every detail of his work. The writer exhorts his readers to have that kind of devotion to understanding the message to which they have been exposed.

The writer makes it clear that they have heard the truth. This is significant in light of the spiritual position of his readers. The original audience of the book of Hebrews were those saved under the old covenant by faith in the Messiah who was to come. If Jesus had not come, they would go to Paradise at the time of death. Now that Jesus has come, and proven himself to be the Messiah, there are two types of devout Jews alive in the first-century: those who have heard of Jesus and his resurrection and those who have not.

Those who have not heard are still under the old covenant and saved by their faith in the promise that a Messiah would come. Those who have heard that salvation is through Jesus, the Messiah who has come, must make a decision.

The author is warning his readers not to pass up this opportunity to receive the truth and the salvation that is in the Jesus described in the past chapter. He warns them not to drift away. This word "pararheo" has the connotation of flowing past. It's a nautical term speaking of a boat that might flow past a safe harbor or a place to dock. In other words, the author does not want them to miss the truth.

His Message Deserves more Careful Obedience

2 For if the message spoken by angels was binding, and every violation and disobedience received its just punishment, 3 how shall we escape if we ignore such a great salvation?

In developing his invitation, the writer of Hebrews

desires to convince his readers of the importance of this message. He does it with an argument from the lesser to the greater. He compares the message spoken by angels to the message of a great salvation. The message spoken by angels is the old covenant in the law while the great salvation is the new covenant in Jesus' blood.

"The message spoken by angels" should likely be translated "the message spoken "through" angels." This is a suitable translation and better reflects the fact that God was the author and proclaimer of the message. The message involved is the law. In the account of the giving of the law in Exodus, chapter twenty, there is no mention of angels. There are, however, texts in both the Old and New Testaments that describe the presence of angels at this event. Moses records the presence of angels when he recaps the time of the Exodus in Deuteronomy 33:

> He said: "The LORD came from Sinai and dawned over them from Seir; he shone forth from Mount Paran. He came with myriads of holy ones from the south, from his mountain slopes. (Deut 33:2)

The Psalmist also acknowledges the presence of angels in the 68th Psalm:

> The chariots of God are tens of thousands and thousands of thousands; the Lord [has come] from Sinai into his sanctuary. (Ps 68:17)

Stephen, the first martyr of the church, also acknowledges the presence of angels in Acts, chapter seven:

> He was in the assembly in the desert, with

the angel who spoke to him on Mount Sinai,
and with our fathers; and he received living
words to pass on to us. (Acts 7:38)

In his same discourse Stephen mentions angels again:

"...you who have received the law that was
put into effect through angels but have not
obeyed it." (Acts 7:53)

The Apostle Paul also speaks of the angel's role in the
giving of the law when he addresses the Galatians church:

What, then, was the purpose of the law? It
was added because of transgressions until the
Seed to whom the promise referred had
come. The law was put into effect through
angels by a mediator.

This message, the law, was so great that it needed to be
mediated by angels. Every violation and disobedience
received its just punishment. The idea of violation is a trans-
gression or "stepping across the line." It encompasses any
sin that is committed. The word disobedience speaks more
of not doing those things which were commanded in other
words, ignoring the commands either through ignorance or
disbelief. Whether sins of commission or omission, they all
received their just punishment.

The point is made that the message of salvation is even
greater than the message spoken through the angels. If this
great salvation is ignored, how shall people escape. In
analyzing this argument from the lesser to the greater many
commentators allude to a greater punishment for those who
ignore salvation than for those who ignored the old
covenant. The text does not support this. The argument

deals with the certainty of punishment as opposed to the degree of punishment. If the old covenant enacted punishment, how can anyone escape the certainty of punishment that will come if this great salvation is ignored.

Ignoring this salvation means rejecting Jesus as the Messiah who has come.

His Message Deserves more Confirmation

This salvation, which was first announced by the Lord, was confirmed to us by those who heard him. 4 God also testified to it by signs, wonders and various miracles, and gifts of the Holy Spirit distributed according to his will.

The author now wants to give additional reasons his readers should receive the message of salvation. His argument includes four confirmations of the message. The first confirmation is that it was announced by the Lord. This is speaking of the Lord Jesus. The fact is that Jesus declared that he was the Messiah. Perhaps some of the Hebrews to whom this book was written thought Jesus was a wonderful Rabbi but not the Messiah. The author is therefore arguing that Jesus made this claim. If Jesus is indeed a good Rabbi or teacher of the Law his message should be accepted. One cannot relegate Jesus to the position of a good teacher and then call his message untrue.

The second confirmation noted that there were eyewitnesses to what Jesus had said. The text says the message "was confirmed to us by those who heard him" this, of course, would speak of the apostles and other followers of Jesus who were still alive at the time of the writing of Hebrews. There were many who could attest to the words of Jesus and also to his bodily resurrection.

The third confirmation of the message deals with signs, wonders, and various miracles. It was appropriate for a prophet to confirm his message with such phenomena. The message of salvation was confirmed in this way by Jesus, as well as by the apostles who followed him.

The fourth confirmation was through gifts of the Spirit. It is uncertain what gifts are in view here. Certain gifts, such as the gift of languages, would seem more likely to be a confirmation of the message. In Apostolic times, when that gift was in operation, it was used to bring truth to the church body. It certainly confirmed the message of salvation through the person of Jesus.

He is a Better Substitute for Mankind   (2:5-9)

5 ¶ It is not to angels that he has subjected the world to come, about which we are speaking. 6 But there is a place where someone has testified: "What is man that you are mindful of him, the son of man that you care for him? 7 You made him a little lower than the angels; you crowned him with glory and honor 8 and put everything under his feet." In putting everything under him, God left nothing that is not subject to him. Yet at present we do not see everything subject to him. 9 But we see Jesus, who was made a little lower than the angels, now crowned with glory and honor because he suffered death, so that by the grace of God he might taste death for everyone.

The invitation has begun, arguments have been offered and now the author puts forth one more compelling reason to put one's faith in Jesus. His argument has to do with the understanding of Psalm 8 verses 4 through 8, which he quotes.

Angels were never Destined to Rule

5 ¶ It is not to angels that he has subjected the world to come, about which we are speaking.

In previous verses the point has already been made that angels were servants. They were never to be those who would rule. The desire of angels to rule, as typified by Lucifer in Isaiah 14, would be considered rebellion and sin that would be judged by the Lord.

From the beginning it was man who was destined to rule. At the time of creation man was told that he would have dominion over the earth. (Gen 1:27-28) This would make mankind even greater than the angels. Through the entrance of sin into the world by the transgressions of Adam and Eve, mankind fell from his exalted position and became lower than the angels.

Man was Demoted from Ruling

6 But there is a place where someone has testified: "'What is man that you are mindful of him, the son of man that you care for him? 7 You made him a little lower than the angels;

While Psalm 8 is clearly a Messianic Psalm, our author first treats it in its normal sense which would be dealing with mankind. He then will apply it to Jesus. The author introduces his quote from Psalm 8 by suggesting "there is a place where someone has testified." This should not be seen as a weakness in the author's handling of Scripture, rather as his confidence in the strength of his readers. They undoubtedly knew this quotation from Psalm 8.

The verse from Psalm 8 that precedes the quoted portion speaks of the vastness of the universe. Compared with that vastness, the psalmist asks, "What is man that thou art mindful of him?" Mankind can seem so insignificant compared to the vastness of the universe.

Psalm 8 relates to the whole of mankind; therefore, the

term "son of man" can simply mean his children. Obviously, in its Messianic application this will be a clear reference to Jesus, the Messiah who has come.

Still quoting from Psalm 8 the author says, "You made him a little lower than the angels." Again this is speaking of mankind. While he was designed to rule, sin caused mankind to be demoted from that position and thereby be made lower than the angels.

Man has been Promised a Future Rule

"You crowned him with glory and honor 8 and put everything under his feet." In putting everything under him, God left nothing that is not subject to him. Yet at present we do not see everything subject to him.

Psalm 8 has a glorious promise for mankind. It speaks of a time when he will be crowned with glory and honor and everything will be put under his feet. In other words, it speaks of a time when he will again have dominion over the earth. There will be nothing that will not be subject to man.

The point is made that presently one does not see everything subject to mankind. There are currently many things that are not subject to man. The greatest of these is death. Through the sin of Adam death entered the world. (Romans 5:12) Man has been subject to death ever since. While man is in subjection to death he cannot be in a position of ruling. At the time of the writing of the book of Hebrews as well as today, we do not see mankind having dominion over the earth and death.

Jesus is the Firstfruits of Man's Future Rule

9 But we see Jesus, who was made a little lower than the angels, now crowned with glory and honor because he suffered death, so that by the grace of God he might taste death for everyone.

But we see Jesus! The author now comes to the crux of the issue and brings his invitation to a close. Everything revolves around Jesus. He shows that Jesus was the man in view in Psalm 8 who was made lower than the angels and is now crowned with glory and honor. Mankind may not yet be crowned with glory and honor but Jesus is. The accounts of his ascension into heaven were available to these Hebrew readers. They knew that he had ascended to the right hand of the father.

The evidence of Jesus' rule is that he suffered death and defeated it. Not only did he suffer his own death, but by the grace of God, he suffered death for everyone.

Having demonstrated dominion over death, Jesus has dominion over everything. He is the firstfruits of the resurrection. Everyone who believes in Jesus will also be crowned with glory and honor as promised in Psalm 8. The invitation is complete. The Hebrews must look to Jesus.

The first nine verses of chapter two have been an invitation. The author has told the Hebrews to pay careful attention to the message and not miss it. He has used an argument from the lesser to the greater to show that if the old covenant law was important, how much more important was the new covenant's great salvation. He has shown that this new covenant was confirmed by the Lord, by eyewitnesses, by signs, wonders, and miracles, and by gifts of the Holy Spirit. He has demonstrated, using Psalm 8, that mankind can only come to his rightful place of glory and honor when death has been defeated. Finally, he offers Jesus as the one who has defeated death and who should be looked to for salvation. It is a call to move from faith in a coming Messiah to faith in Jesus, the Messiah who has come.

Chapter Six

Jesus is a Brother, Superior
to God's Children   (2:10 to 2:18)

He is a Better Author of Salvation
for Mankind   (2:10-13)

10 In bringing many sons to glory, it was fitting that God, for whom and through whom everything exists, should make the author of their salvation perfect through suffering. 11 Both the one who makes men holy and those who are made holy are of the same family. So Jesus is not ashamed to call them brothers. 12 He says, "I will declare your name to my brothers; in the presence of the congregation I will sing your praises." 13 And again, "I will put my trust in him." And again he says, "Here am I, and the children God has given me."

In the previous verse it was concluded that Jesus had suffered death and tasted death for everyone. The idea that Jesus was a substitute for all mankind is now developed. There could be no better substitute for mankind than Jesus.

The Hebrews of Jesus' day had been looking for an "author of their salvation;" however, their expectation was for a great military leader to usher in the kingdom. Jesus came instead as the suffering servant. This certainly could be a disappointment and a stumbling block to the Hebrews.

The author now turns his attention to demonstrating that it was fitting for God to bring salvation in precisely the way he did. He demonstrates that every action was consistent with the character of God.

He was Perfected Through Suffering

10 In bringing many sons to glory, it was fitting that God, for whom and through whom everything exists, should make the author of their salvation perfect through suffering.

The expectations of the Hebrews for a Messiah was that he would bring many sons to glory. The author of Hebrews shows that God's choice of how to do that was fitting. By nature, God is holy and his law is holy. His nature would therefore demand death to those who violated the law. He could not simply come to earth and abolish the law. That would be inconsistent with his nature. Instead he sent his Son to be the payment for the violations of law.

The Son was the spotless sacrificial lamb that satisfied the wrath of God. The Son through his resurrection also annulled the power of Satan. In addition, the Son's experience enabled him to be a compassionate high priest. All of this is fitting and consistent with the nature of God.

MacArthur concludes:

> What he did was consistent with his holiness for God showed on the cross his hatred for sin. It was consistent with his power, being the greatest display of power ever manifested. Christ endured for a few hours what will take an eternity for unrepentant sinners to endure. It was consistent with his love, in that he loved the world so much that he gave his only Son for its redemption. Finally, what he did was consistent with his grace, because Christ's sacrifice was substitutionary. The work of salvation was totally consistent with God's nature. It was entirely fitting for him to have done what he did. (MacArthur p 66)

It was also consistent with the nature of God that he would redeem mankind. The author states that everything exists through God and for God. To have lost mankind would imply that they did not exist for him. It was always God's plan that mankind would bring glory to him. His actions have brought mankind back into a position of worship to the one for whom everything exists. (Col 1:15-20)

Jesus is next described as the author of their salvation. The Greek word author is "archegos" which literally means a pioneer or leader. In other words, Jesus is the one who has led the way to salvation. This is consistent with his claim in the upper room:

> Jesus answered, "I am the way and the truth and the life. No one comes to the Father except through me." (John 14:6)

Through his suffering, Jesus was perfected. This is not to say that Jesus had some defect that needed to be worked out. It is rather that his perfection was demonstrated by the acceptance of his sacrifice. If Jesus were not a suitable sacrifice, he could never have defeated death and the resurrection never would have occurred. His perfection was demonstrated through his suffering, death and resurrection. Without that experience, his perfection would not have been exhibited to mankind.

He is An Unashamed Brother

11 Both the one who makes men holy and those who are made holy are of the same family. So Jesus is not ashamed to call them brothers. 12 He says, "I will declare your name to my brothers; in the presence of the congregation I will sing your praises."

"The one who makes men holy" is a reference to Jesus. This is consistent with the teaching of Hebrews in chapter ten:

> And by that will, we have been made holy through the sacrifice of the body of Jesus Christ once-for-all. (Heb 10:10)

And again in verse 14:

> because by one sacrifice he has made perfect forever those who are being made holy. (Heb 10:14)

Those who are made holy are the ones for whom Jesus died, specifically, those who would put their faith and trust in Jesus Christ as Savior. The believer's holiness is positional as opposed to practical. Believers are righteous before God, even though they continue to sin. It is Christ's righteousness that has value, not the righteousness of individual believers.

The suggestion that Jesus and believers are of the same family is interesting. At Jesus' birth he was made part of the family of mankind. At each man's new birth he is made part of the family of God. In both senses, Jesus and the believer are part of the same family.

Next, the author informs his readers that Jesus is not ashamed to call them brothers. To think that Jesus would be proud of a relationship with mankind is paradoxical at best. Certainly, believers should be proud to have Jesus as a brother, but his being ashamed of sinful brothers would seem appropriate. Instead, Jesus is not ashamed to call believers brothers, yet he knows that there are times when believers are ashamed of him.

In the earliest conversation following Jesus' resurrection

he referred to the redeemed as his brothers. He met Mary in the garden:

> Jesus said, "Do not hold on to me, for I have not yet returned to the Father. Go instead to my brothers and tell them, 'I am returning to my Father and your Father, to my God and your God.'" (John 20:17)

The author of Hebrews again appeals to a Messianic Psalm to show that Jesus' behavior is consistent with that of the Messiah who was to come. Psalm 22 is clearly Messianic and includes the reference that says the Messiah will declare your name to my brothers. Once again it is observed that the redeemed are called brothers of the Messiah. The expression "in the presence of the congregation" uses the word "ecclesia" for congregation. This word, meaning "assembly" is usually translated "church" in the New Testament. In this context "congregation" was used since it was a quote from Psalm 22. Obviously, the church was not in view in the Old Testament so the word would have implied "congregation" or "assembly." In translation, it makes sense to preserve "congregation" rather than changing it to "church." In practical terms, however, it is in the church that Psalm 22 finds its fulfillment.

He is A Trusting Son

13 And again, "I will put my trust in him." And again he says, "here am I, and the children God has given me."

The author now quotes from Isaiah, chapter eight. In its context, Ahaz was the king of Judah and made an agreement with the Assyrians because of an impending invasion by Rezin King of Aram and Pekah King of Israel. (2 Kings

16:7-8) The king had put his trust in an alliance with the Assyrians. At this time, Isaiah proclaims that he put his trust in God. He offers his children as signs from the Lord:

> Here am I, and the children the LORD has given me. We are signs and symbols in Israel from the LORD Almighty, who dwells on Mount Zion.

The names of Isaiah's children are Shear-Jashub which means "a remnant shall return" and Mahershalalhashbaz, which means "quick to the plunder, swift to the spoil." These names, coupled with the profession of trust by Isaiah, demonstrate his confidence in God to preserve a remnant. At the time when Isaiah proclaimed judgment, he also gave this prophetic message of hope and confidence in the Lord. Both Isaiah and the children God had given him shared the common trust.

The writer to the Hebrews, having just talked about Jesus and believers being of one family now quotes these verses. His point is that both Jesus and believers had to put their trust in the living God. Jesus, in his humanity, became weak and needed perfect dependence upon the father. Likewise, the Hebrews would have to become weak and have perfect dependence upon God.

The Hebrew audience could no longer be saved by an old covenant, its sacrificial system, and its promise of a Messiah to come. They now had to be one of the children given to Jesus in order to be saved. This is consistent with the teaching of Jesus as recorded in the book of John:

> "All that the Father gives me will come to me, and whoever comes to me I will never drive away. For I have come down from heaven not to do my will but to do the will of

him who sent me. And this is the will of him who sent me, that I shall lose none of all that he has given me, but raise them up at the last day. For my Father's will is that everyone who looks to the Son and believes in him shall have eternal life, and I will raise him up at the last day." (John 6:37-40)

It could not be clearer that the Hebrews had to turn to Jesus the son to be saved.

He is a Better Conqueror of the Devil   (2:14-16)

14 ¶ Since the children have flesh and blood, he too shared in their humanity so that by his death he might destroy him who holds the power of death—that is, the devil— 15 and free those who all their lives were held in slavery by their fear of death. 16 For surely it is not angels he helps, but Abraham's descendants.

In chapter two, verse nine, the author of Hebrews made the point that Jesus was crowned with glory and honor because he suffered death both for himself and for others. Jesus conquest over death not only brought him glory and honor but also had an impact on the devil and his power. Jesus resurrection to new life defeated death and saved mankind.

He Shared in Humanity & Death

14 ¶ Since the children have flesh and blood, he too shared in their humanity so that by his death he might destroy him who holds the power of death—that is, the devil—

This verse begins "the children have flesh and blood." The word translated "have" comes from the Greek "koinonia." This is the common word for "fellowship" and implies that people have something in common. All mankind shares the commonality of flesh and blood. The verse maintains that he (Jesus) too shared in their humanity. The word "shared" in reference to Jesus is the Greek word "metecho." This word means "to take hold of something that is not naturally one's own." It is used elsewhere in Hebrews to speak of mankind "sharing in the heavenly calling":

> Therefore, holy brothers, who share (metecho) in the heavenly calling, fix your thoughts on Jesus, the apostle and high priest whom we confess. (Heb 3:1)

It is also used of mankind's sharing in Christ:

> We have come to share (metecho) in Christ if we hold firmly till the end the confidence we had at first. (Heb 3:14)

It is also used of sharing in the Holy Spirit:

> It is impossible for those who have once been enlightened, who have tasted the heavenly gift, who have shared (metecho) in the Holy Spirit,... (Heb 6:4)

In each use it is something that believers take hold of that is not natural, just as here Jesus took hold of humanity which is not part of his original nature.

Jesus did this for the specific purpose of dying. When sin entered the world, the penalty was death. It is that penalty that has given the devil power over mankind. He knows that the soul that sinneth, it shall die.(Ez 18:4) God made the rule but Satan has used it as his most powerful weapon.

Jesus died so that he could rob Satan of this death-weapon. Jesus has a weapon far more powerful. It is eternal life. When Jesus rose from the dead, he destroyed the power of death and thereby robbed Satan of his weapon, resulting in Satan's certain defeat.

He Freed Man from the Fear of Death

15 and free those who all their lives were held in slavery by their fear of death.

Mankind's greatest fear, and greatest enemy is death. Death implies eternal separation from God and eternal punishment. Even the greatest of fools would fear such a destiny. The text suggests that mankind is held in slavery by this fear.

When Jesus died and then rose, he defeated death. The Apostle Paul rejoices with the rhetorical question, "Oh death, where is your sting?" (1 Cor 15:55) Because Jesus tasted death for all mankind (Heb 2:9) there is no fear of death for those who believe.

He Helped Mankind

16 For surely it is not angels he helps, but Abraham's descendants.

The author reminds his readers that the conquering of death was not to help angels but to help Abraham's descendants. Angels already possess eternal life, unless they were among those who followed Satan, in which case there is no help for them, only eternal damnation. Abraham's descendants, that is, mankind, are the ones for whom Jesus died and destroyed the power of the devil.

The word translated "helps" is "epilambano"; it also has the meaning "to take hold of." It is used most frequently of grabbing something to save it. The word usage is extremely well illustrated in Matthew's account of Peter's walking on the water:

> "Lord, if it's you," Peter replied, "tell me to come to you on the water." "Come," he said. Then Peter got down out of the boat, walked on the water and came towards Jesus. But when he saw the wind, he was afraid and, beginning to sink, cried out, "Lord, save me!" Immediately Jesus reached out his hand and caught him (epilambano). "You of little faith," he said, "why did you doubt?" (Matt 14:28-31)

When Jesus reached out his hand and "caught" Peter the word used is "epilambano." Jesus saved Peter from drowning. Likewise in the usage of the word in Hebrews, chapter two, Jesus grabs mankind and saves them from death. The idea is far more then just giving some help to Abraham's descendants, it clearly implies saving those descendants from eternal death.

He is a Better High Priest in Service to God (2:17-18)

> 17 For this reason he had to be made like his brothers in every way, in order that he might become a merciful and faithful high priest in service to God, and that he might make

atonement for the sins of the people. 18
Because he himself suffered when he was
tempted, he is able to help those who are
being tempted.

In order to pay the penalty for mankind's sin and effectively defeat death, Jesus had to be an acceptable sacrifice.
When a Hebrew believer, saved under the old covenant,
would bring his lamb to the temple, he would bring one
without spot or blemish. It needed to be an appropriate
sacrifice.

Jesus is the lamb of God that takes away the sin of the
world. In order to be the perfect sacrifice, he had to become
a man, be tempted, yet without sin, and be willing to make
atonement for the sins of the people. Jesus was not only the
sacrifice but also the high priest in service to God.

He was Made Like his Brothers

*17 For this reason he had to be made like his brothers in every
way, in order that he might become a merciful and faithful high
priest in service to God,*

The use of the word "brothers" here implies that Jesus
became like humanity. It is obvious that the use of the term
"brothers" in this context does not mean Christians. Those
who generally conclude that the term "brothers" always
refers to Christians would not insist on it in this context.
That sets a good stage for the beginning of chapter three
where brothers is used and does not necessarily mean
Christians, either.

In becoming like his brothers, Jesus not only put on
flesh and blood, but he experienced humanity in every way.
MacArthur has a good summary:

He was hungry, he was thirsty, he was overcome with fatigue, he slept, he was taught, he grew, he loved, he was astonished, he was glad, he was angry, he was indignant, he was sarcastic, he was grieved, he was troubled, he was overcome by future events, he exercised faith, he read the Scriptures, he prayed, he sighed in his heart when he saw another man in illness, and he cried when his heart ached. (MacArthur p 71)

The text tells us that the purpose for Jesus' experiencing all of this was that he might become a merciful and faithful high priest in service to God. In the Old Testament economy, the prophet was the one who brought the word of the Lord to the people. The high priest, on the other hand, was the one who brought the people to God. He was the one who presented the annual sacrifice to make atonement for the sins of the people.

By virtue of his sacrifice on the cross of Calvary, Jesus became not only the sacrifice but also the high priest who presents the sacrifice before God. He is said to be a merciful and faithful high priest. "Merciful" is a reference to the way he deals with the sinners whom he represents and their human need. "Faithfulness" is a reference to how he deals with the father and the divine requirements of holiness. Jesus is both merciful and faithful.

Because Jesus has experienced everything that mankind has experienced he is capable of sympathy. He understands mankind's weakness when dealing with temptation.

He was Able to Atone for Sins

and that he might make atonement for the sins of the people.

Having become a merciful and faithful high priest, Jesus was able to make atonement for the sins of the people. The word translated "atonement" is rendered "propitiation" by other translators. Propitiation is the act of satisfying the wrath of God, which is to say, meeting the demands of his own holiness. Jesus as high priest did not convince God not to be mad about sin any more. Instead, he brought into the holy place a suitable sacrifice, that is, himself. God's wrath had been poured out on Jesus during his crucifixion. God did not set aside his wrath in order to be merciful. He rather took his wrath upon himself in order to show mercy to mankind.

He is Able to Help Those Being Tempted

18 Because he himself suffered when he was tempted, he is able to help those who are being tempted.

When Jesus dwelt among mankind he was tempted in every way yet he was without sin. The writer describes his enduring of temptation as suffering. Inasmuch as Jesus could not sin, one wonders how much he really suffered in temptation. The answer is that he suffered much more than any individual on the face of the earth could suffer. This is so for two reasons. First, he would have to have been the focus of Satan's greatest attacks. If Satan convinced Jesus to sin, all mankind would be forever lost.

The second reason his suffering was so intense is because he did not succumb to temptation. If resisting temptation is suffering, as soon as an individual stops resisting the suffering ceases. Mankind, with his tendency towards sin, stops resisting as the intensity and duration of temptation increases. Jesus, on the other hand, never stopped resisting, despite the intensity and duration of any temptation that came his way. He took all that Satan could offer and did not sin.

Because Jesus is aware of the nature of temptation and because he was able to defeat it, he is able to help others who are being tempted. In this instance the word "help" is "boetheo", which means "to succor" or "to come to the aid of." It is a word that implies someone is coming alongside to assist in a struggle. When one is being tempted, Jesus is willing to be invited into the struggle as a brother who is superior to all of God's children. He wants to help his brothers in their times of need.

Chapter Seven

Jesus is a Prophet
Superior to Moses   (3:1 to 4:13)

He is a Better House Builder
for the Holy   (3:1-6)

1 ¶ Therefore, holy brothers, who share in the heavenly calling, fix your thoughts on Jesus, the apostle and high priest whom we confess. 2 He was faithful to the one who appointed him, just as Moses was faithful in all God's house. 3 Jesus has been found worthy of greater honor than Moses, just as the builder of a house has greater honor than the house itself. 4 For every house is built by someone, but God is the builder of everything. 5 Moses was faithful as a servant in all God's house, testifying to what would be said in the future. 6 But Christ is faithful as a son over God's house. And we are his house, if we hold on to our courage and the hope of which we boast.

At this point, the author turns his audience's attention to two highly acclaimed individuals of the old covenant. They are Moses the prophet and Aaron the high priest. The author spends a brief time demonstrating Jesus' superiority to Moses and then spends several chapters dealing with Jesus' role as a superior high priest. In his discussion of these particular individuals, the author of Hebrews makes it absolutely clear that Jesus is the Messiah who was to come and that the Hebrews should put their faith in him.

The Apostle and High Priest of our Confession

1 ¶ Therefore, holy brothers, who share in the heavenly calling, fix your thoughts on Jesus, the apostle and high priest whom we confess.

The NIV translation of this text provides a word order that tends to be interpretive rather than just grammatical. In order to avoid drawing conclusions based on the NIV translation, it is important to deal with the text in its original word order. The New King James version is truer to the text:

> Therefore, holy brethren, partakers of the heavenly calling, consider the apostle and high priest of our confession, Christ Jesus (Heb 3:1 NKJV).

Having presented a more appropriate word order the text may now be examined with greater objectivity and understanding. It begins with the word "therefore" which ties this section into what has gone before it. The author has just demonstrated that Jesus is a superior brother, that he suffered temptation, that he was without sin, and that he made atonement for the sins of people. In light of that, our author wants the holy brethren to consider their confession.

He calls them holy brothers who share in the heavenly calling. At first consideration, one might conclude that these are believers in Christ. In a sense they are; they are believers in the Christ (the Messiah) who is to come. They are not yet believers in Jesus. They, like the author of Hebrews, have been saved under the old covenant, believing in a Messiah who was to come. They are holy brothers in the same sense as Paul speaks of in Romans 9:

> For I could wish that I myself were cursed

and cut off from Christ for the sake of my
brothers, those of my own race, the people of
Israel. Theirs is the adoption as sons; theirs
the divine glory, the covenants, the receiving
of the law, the temple worship and the
promises. Theirs are the patriarchs, and from
them is traced the human ancestry of Christ,
who is God over all, forever praised! Amen.
(Rom 9:3-5)

In this text, Paul refers to the people of Israel as his
brothers and speaks of the wonderful benefits that are part
of their confession of faith as the people of God. They
certainly were sharers in a heavenly calling throughout the
Old Testament.

The writer to the Hebrews, referring to his Israelite
brothers, reminds them that they are partakers in the heavenly calling. They have been called to faith in the coming
Messiah.

In light of their position as holy brothers and sharers in a
heavenly calling, he now encourages them to consider their
confession. There are two aspects of their confession in
view here. The first is as an apostle the second as a high
priest. The word "apostle" means "one who is sent." The
Hebrews were looking for one to be sent from God. This
would be a prophet like Moses:

The LORD your God will raise up for you a
prophet like me from among your own brothers. You must listen to him. For this is what
you asked of the LORD your God at Horeb
on the day of the assembly when you said,
"Let us not hear the voice of the LORD our
God nor see this great fire any more, or we
will die." The LORD said to me: "What they

say is good. I will raise up for them a prophet like you from among their brothers; I will put my words in his mouth, and he will tell them everything I command him. If anyone does not listen to my words that the prophet speaks in my name, I myself will call him to account.(Duet 18:15-19)

The Hebrews would also confess their faith in a high priest who was to come:

"'The days are coming,' declares the LORD, 'when I will fulfill the gracious promise I made to the house of Israel and to the house of Judah. "'In those days and at that time I will make a righteous Branch sprout from David's line; he will do what is just and right in the land. In those days Judah will be saved and Jerusalem will live in safety. This is the name by which it will be called: The LORD Our Righteousness.' For this is what the LORD says: 'David will never fail to have a man to sit on the throne of the house of Israel, nor will the priests, who are Levites, ever fail to have a man to stand before me continually tò offer burnt offerings, to burn grain offerings and to present sacrifices.'" (Jeremiah 33:14-18)

The author is suggesting that they consider their confession. He includes himself when he calls it "our confession." He can do this because the confession is true: there is an apostle (prophet) who was promised and there is a high priest who was promised.

If a period was placed here—and it certainly could be—

the next sentence would be, "Jesus (or Christ Jesus according to NKJV) was faithful to the one who appointed him..." This is consistent with the Greek text since the word "He" that begins verse 2 is not in the text but is assumed from the construction of the verb "was". If "Jesus" is substituted for the word "He" the verb construction continues to be correct. The resulting suggested translation is:

> Therefore, holy brothers, who share in the heavenly calling, fix your thoughts on the apostle and high priest of our confession. Jesus was faithful to the one who appointed him, just as Moses was faithful in all God's house. (Heb 3:1-2 Translation from Greek)

The first sentence tells the Hebrews to consider their confession; the second sentence presents Jesus as the one who is the fulfillment of that confession. This is consistent with the chapters that will follow. He first compares Jesus to Moses, demonstrating that he is the prophet like unto Moses. Then he spends several chapters comparing Jesus to Aaron and demonstrating that he is the high priest who was promised. Even without Jesus' being a Levite, the author supports the legal right for Jesus to be the high priest.

Once the author has demonstrated that Jesus is both the prophet and high priest who was to come, he will have firmly established the argument that the Hebrews should place their faith in Jesus Christ, the one who was to come.

Moses was a Faithful Member of God's House

2 He was faithful to the one who appointed him, just as Moses was faithful in all God's house.

The author begins with a simple comparison of Jesus to

Moses. Moses was known for his faithfulness in following God. The same God who appointed Moses to be a servant of God's house at the burning bush, was the God who appointed Jesus to be the son over God's house.

Jesus is the Faithful Builder of God's House

3 Jesus has been found worthy of greater honor than Moses, just as the builder of a house has greater honor than the house itself. 4 For every house is built by someone, but God is the builder of everything.

The author suggests that Jesus has been found worthy of greater honor than Moses. The greater honor had already been identified in chapter two, verse nine:

> But we see Jesus, who was made a little lower than the angels, now crowned with glory and honor because he suffered death, so that by the grace of God he might taste death for everyone. (Heb 2:9)

Jesus was crowned with glory and honor because he suffered death and was ultimately raised from the dead. Therein lies the difference. Jesus conquered death, whereas the book of Joshua tells us:

> "Moses my servant is dead." (Joshua 1:2)

Moses and the other believing Hebrews were part of the house being built by God. The key to an enduring house built by God is eternal life. Jesus, through his atoning death, became the provider of eternal life and the builder of the house.

The author also makes the point that God is the builder

of everything. He has previously expounded the idea that Jesus is God when in chapter one, verse eight, he attributed Psalm 104 to Jesus. This Psalm calls the Messiah God.

Moses was Faithful in God's House

5 Moses was faithful as a servant in all God's house, testifying to what would be said in the future.

Moses, as God's prophet, spoke on his behalf. He was faithful in that he spoke those things that God wanted him to. Often his prophecies would include information about the future. Moses was faithful to deliver that information regardless of how difficult it might have been for people to comprehend.

Christ is Faithful Over God's House

6 But Christ is faithful as a son over God's house. And we are his house, if we hold on to our courage and the hope of which we boast.

The author now compares Christ as being faithful as a son over God's house. In John, chapter six, Jesus is comparing himself to events of Moses' day. He declares, "I am the bread of life." This is in contrast to the bread from heaven of Moses day. Jesus then makes the point of saying, "For I have come down from heaven not to do my will but to do the will of him who sent me." (John 6:38) Jesus was clearly faithful to the father, testifying what the father chose for him to say.

The author of Hebrews now brings his audience to a point of decision. They believe they are part of God's house. There is a hope of which they boast and in which they take courage. Once again, our author includes himself by saying it is a hope in which "we boast." The obvious question is, "What is that hope?" The answer was already given in verse one. It is the apostle and high priest of their confession.

Their belief and confession that there would come a prophet like unto Moses and a high priest like unto Aaron was the source of their courage and hope. In other words, their faith in the coming Messiah was their source of courage and hope. The author has skillfully demonstrated that Jesus is the Messiah who has come. If the Hebrews miss that reality, they have thereby discarded their courage and hope. They must see the truth in order to hold on to their courage and hope.

The author now looks back to the days of Moses in the wilderness to demonstrate the peril of discarding their courage and hope through disbelief.

The Holy Spirit Warns Against Disbelieving God's Message   (3:7-14)

7 ¶ So, as the Holy Spirit says: "Today, if you hear his voice, 8 do not harden your hearts as you did in the rebellion, during the time of testing in the desert, 9 where your fathers tested and tried me and for forty years saw what I did. 10 That is why I was angry with that generation, and I said, 'Their hearts are always going astray, and they have not known my ways.' 11 So I declared on oath in my anger, 'They shall never enter my rest. 12 See to it, brothers, that none of you has a sinful, unbelieving heart that turns away from the living God. 13 But encourage one another daily, as long as it is called Today, so that none of you may be hardened by sin's deceitfulness. 14 We have come to share in Christ if we hold firmly till the end the confidence we had at first.

The author of Hebrews now presents some stern warnings. In doing so, he refers to the forty year period during the Exodus from Egypt. He draws clear parallels between the Israelites of the Exodus and the Hebrews of the first-century.

The first-century Hebrews were also in the midst of a forty year period. It began at the time of Jesus death and resurrection, which ushered in the new covenant in 30 AD. It ends with the destruction of the temple and the old covenant sacrificial system in 70 AD. During that forty year window of opportunity, those who were saved under the old covenant by trusting in a coming Messiah would have the opportunity to place that trust in the Messiah who has come.

The example of the Israelites in the wilderness allows the author of Hebrews to demonstrate just what a heart of unbelief is capable of. This gives him the backdrop to sternly warn the first-century Hebrews not to fall prey to such unbelief.

The Example of the Israelites During 40 Years in the Past

7 ¶ So, as the Holy Spirit says: "Today, if you hear his voice, 8 do not harden your hearts as you did in the rebellion, during the time of testing in the desert, 9 where your fathers tested and tried me and for forty years saw what I did. 10 That is why I was angry with that generation, and I said, 'Their hearts are always going astray, and they have not known my ways.' 11 So I declared on oath in my anger, 'They shall never enter my rest.'"

The author's first example is presented utilizing a quotation from Psalm 95, verses 7 through 11. This Psalm was written by David, yet the author of Hebrews attributes it to the Holy Spirit. This is one of the clearest evidences for inspiration of Scripture, both Old and New Testament.

David was utilizing the example of the Israelites in the

Exodus to warn the people of his day. The writer of Hebrews used it to warn the first-century Hebrews. The warnings also are applicable to any day prior to the coming of the Lord Jesus Christ in judgment. The passage begins "Today." This does not imply a twenty four hour period but rather the present moment. Paul's writing to the church at Corinth gives the sense of what "today" means:

> For he says, "In the time of my favor I heard you, and in the day of salvation I helped you." I tell you, now is the time of God's favor, now is the day of salvation. (2 Cor 6:2)

"Day" is the "day of salvation." It is the day to turn to the Messiah, Jesus.

In the immediate context, the antecedent of the pronoun "his" would be found in verse six "Christ." This, of course, is the Hebrew word for the Messiah. It is also the same person as was identified in verse three, that is, "Jesus." When David wrote this Psalm, the antecedent of the pronoun "his" came from the previous verses of the Psalm which said "the Lord our maker, he is our God." The writer of Hebrews is asserting that the Messiah (Jesus) is the Lord and is God.

There are a number of significant observations to be made concerning this example of belief. Concerning hearing God's voice there is little question that all the Israelites at the time of the Exodus heard his voice. It bellowed from Mount Sinai and frightened them all. In the metaphorical sense they also heard his voice as they witnessed the many miracles that he performed during their wilderness wanderings.

They hardened their hearts. The word "heart" is a term frequently used in Hebrew poetry. It can mean a number of things such as the blood pumping muscle, the emotions, the soul, the mind, and the will. In the context of the wilderness the word "heart" likely refers to the will. The Israelites had a choice to believe God or not. That choice certainly would be influenced by the mind and emotions but ultimately it was a decision of the will that would bring them to complete faith and trust in God. Their wills were hardened and they refused to believe.

They tested God. The context of the testing can be found in Exodus, chapter seventeen:

> The whole Israelite community set out from the Desert of Sin, traveling from place to place as the LORD commanded. They camped at Rephidim, but there was no water for the people to drink. So they quarreled with Moses and said, "Give us water to drink." Moses replied, "Why do you quarrel with me? Why do you put the LORD to the test?" But the people were thirsty for water there, and they grumbled against Moses. They said, "Why did you bring us up out of Egypt to make us and our children and live-stock die of thirst?" Then Moses cried out to the LORD, "What am I to do with these people? They are almost ready to stone me." The LORD answered Moses, "Walk on ahead of the people. Take with you some of the elders of Israel and take in your hand the staff with which you struck the Nile, and go. I will stand there before you by the rock at Horeb. Strike the rock, and water will come out of it for the people to drink." So Moses did this in the sight of the elders of Israel. And he called the place Massah and Meribah because the Israelites quarreled and because they tested the LORD saying, "Is the LORD

among us or not?"(Ex 17:1-7)

Notice that the core of the problem is expressed in the question, "Is the Lord among us or not?" That is the identical question being asked by the first-century Hebrews. They have been expecting a Messiah; Jesus has arrived; is he the one? The writer of Hebrews desires his audience to accept the truth that Jesus is the Lord.

The Israelites ignored what they witnessed. For forty years they saw miracles in the desert yet refused to believe that the Lord was among them. Likewise, the first-century Hebrews were experiencing miracles during their forty year window of opportunity. In addition to the miracles performed by Jesus during his three years of ministry, they saw numerous miracles and healings by the apostles, as well as other manifestations of the gifts of the Holy Spirit.

The Israelites drew wrong conclusions. Despite all the evidence presented to the Israelites of the Exodus, they still did not know the ways of the Lord. They examined the evidence but did not come to the right conclusions. During the first century, the Hebrews likewise examined evidence. The exhortation was that they draw the right conclusions.

The Israelites angered God. Since God presented such overwhelming evidence of his being among them, he was rightfully angered when that evidence was rejected.

The Israelites forfeited the rest. They were headed for a promised land that was to be a land of rest. Had they faithfully followed the Lord and believed his promises they would have entered such a land of rest. Even though the descendants entered Canaan forty years later, it was not a land of rest. It was a land of wars and invasions. The very existence of the Israelites was threatened by the Assyrians, the Babylonians, and the Romans as well as many lesser kingdoms.

The Exhortations to the Hebrews
Concerning 40 Years in the Present

12 See to it, brothers, that none of you has a sinful, unbeliev-ing heart that turns away from the living God. 13 But encour-age one another daily, as long as it is called Today, so that none of you may be hardened by sin's deceitfulness. 14 We have come to share in Christ if we hold firmly till the end the confi-dence we had at first.

Based on the example of the Exodus Israelites, the writer to the Hebrews gives three clear exhortations. First, do not have an unbelieving heart. The heart of unbelief is described as sinful. Often, in contemporary times, when an invitation to receive Jesus as personal savior is given, it is presented as if an individual has a choice. The reality is that there is not a Biblical invitation to believe but rather a Biblical command to believe. Anything short of belief is sin.

The unbelieving heart is also characterized as turning away from the living God. This is the same issue that was being dealt with in Exodus 17: "Is the Lord among us or not?" Failure of the first-century Hebrews to believe that Jesus was the Messiah means that they were turning away from the living God.

The second exhortation is to encourage one another. They should encourage each other to carefully examine the claims being made by Christ, the apostles and, particularly, the writer to the Hebrews. They should encourage one another to believe God. The time to do that is described as "Today." This, of course, gives the sense of urgency. They should make their decision immediately. In view is the window of opportunity given to the first-century Hebrews. The forty years from 30 AD to 70 AD was their "today." Everything was going to change in 70 AD when the temple would be destroyed. The author of Hebrews may have had some insights into what was going to happen. In chapter eight, verse thirteen, he speaks of the old covenant being obsolete and aging and makes the statement that it will soon disappear.

Part of encouraging each other included avoiding the deception of sin. Sin is deceitful. It can make taking the wrong path or making the wrong decision seem correct. The Hebrews were to encourage each other to seek that which was true.

The third exhortation is to hold the course. They started well by believing that there was a Messiah who was to come. They will only get to share in that Messiah (Christ) if they hold their confidence to the end. The confidence spoken of was their faith in God's plan that a Messiah would come. In their time, there was much about Jesus that did not fit their preconceived notions concerning the Messiah. The Israelites in the wilderness wanted God to do things their way, as opposed to his. Likewise, the Hebrews would have preferred God to do things differently. The reality is, if they didn't accept God's plan, then they could not have the Messiah.

Their confidence was waning because they weren't pleased with the current plan. The author of Hebrews is encouraging them to have confidence in what God was doing—the same confidence they had when they first believed his plan for a coming Messiah. They must not turn from God, rather confidently believe in this next phase of his plan which involves the person of Jesus.

The Holy Spirit Warns Against Presuming on God's Grace (3:15-4:3a)

15 As has just been said: "Today, if you hear his voice, do not harden your hearts as you did in the rebellion." 16 Who were they who heard and rebelled? Were they not all those Moses led out of Egypt? 17 And with whom was he angry for forty years? Was it not with those who sinned, whose bodies fell in the desert? 18 And to whom did God swear that they would never enter his rest if not to those who disobeyed? 19 So we see that they were not able to enter, because of their unbelief. 1 ¶ Therefore, since the promise of entering his rest still stands, let us be careful that none of you be found to have fallen short of it. 2 For we also have had the gospel preached to us, just as they did; but the message they heard was of no value to them, because those who heard did not combine it with faith. 3 Now we who have believed enter that rest, just as God has said, "So I declared on oath in my anger, 'They shall never enter my rest.'" And yet his work has been finished since the creation of the world.

Having finished warning the Hebrews not to disbelieve God's message, the author now warns them not to presume on God's grace. There was a great deal of confidence in being a Jew, particularly one who was zealous for the Lord, saved under the old covenant, and looking for the consolation of Israel, the Messiah. The author of Hebrews now draws parallels to the Exodus to show that such confidence is presumptuous, unless they believe in Jesus.

The Example of the Israelites During 40 Years in the Past

15 As has just been said: "Today, if you hear his voice, do not harden your hearts as you did in the rebellion." 16 Who were they who heard and rebelled? Were they not all those Moses led out of Egypt? 17 And with whom was he angry for forty years? Was it not with those who sinned, whose bodies fell in the desert? 18 And to whom did God swear that they would never enter his rest if not to those who disobeyed? 19 So we see that they were not able to enter, because of their unbelief.

In returning to the same example of the Exodus, the author again exhorts his audience not to harden their hearts as the Israelites did. He then presents a logical progression of the Israelites' failure to enter the promised rest.

To begin with, they were all with Moses. The fact that Moses led them all out of Egypt to the Red Sea and provided for them in the wilderness could give the mistaken impression that they were right with God. It is presumptuous to think that one is right with God because one is part of the correct group. Being with a godly man like Moses was not sufficient. Likewise, the Hebrews of the first-century would not find their salvation by being part of the synagogue, even though there were many zealous Hebrews there. Even today, joining the right group does not make an individual right with God.

The author next makes the point that those very people angered God because of sin. During the forty years all of them except Joshua and Caleb would die in the wilderness. This is a clear example that the wages of sin is death. (Rom 3:23)

The sin resulted from disobedience. The text reveals that God would not let them enter his rest because they disobeyed. An important question is, "What was the nature of their disobedience?" The answer is provided in verse nineteen, "So we see they were not able to enter because of their unbelief." In these two verses disobedience is equated with disbelief. God was not looking for the Israelites to do anything on his behalf. He was instead requiring that they trust him to do things on their behalf. If they did not believe God they were disobedient and sinful and would die. The first-century Hebrews wanted to do many things on God's behalf. All he wanted from them was to believe what he did on their behalf. He sent his son, the Messiah, to die for them at Calvary. Failure to believe that Jesus was the Messiah who had come was disobedience to God, sin, and a cause for death.

The Exhortations to the Hebrews
Concerning 40 Years in the Present

1 ¶ Therefore, since the promise of entering his rest still stands, let us be careful that none of you be found to have fallen short of it. 2 For we also have had the gospel preached to us, just as they did; but the message they heard was of no value to them, because those who heard did not combine it with faith. 3 Now we who have believed enter that rest, just as God has said, "So I declared on oath in my anger, 'They shall never enter my rest.'" And yet his work has been finished since the creation of the world.

The author now draws the parallels between the Exodus Israelites and the first-century Hebrews. He again reminds them that the time is now. The promise of entering his rest still stands. The rest at this point is more than entrance into the promised land, rather an eternal rest that can be theirs if they believe God.

The next verse is quite revealing about the author and his relationship to the audience. He says, "Let us be careful." As has been his practice throughout the letter, he includes himself with his brother Israelites by using the word "us". This changes, however, as he completes the sentence. He says, "Let us be careful that none of you be found to have fallen short of it." He excludes himself from one who is in danger of falling short of the rest. He does this because he believes the message and has accepted the plan that Jesus is the one who was to come. When one receives Jesus Christ as his Savior, there is confidence in one's eternal destiny. The reason the Hebrews could fall short of the rest was previously given in chapter three, verse nineteen; that reason is unbelief. The book of Hebrews was written to persuade those saved under the old covenant, looking for the Messiah to come, that Jesus was the Messiah who had come. Unbelief in that plan and the person of Jesus would result in their falling short of the rest.

The author goes on and makes his point abundantly clear. He reminds his readers that they have heard the Gospel message. Just as those in the wilderness heard the good news God had for them, likewise, the first-century Hebrews heard the good news that God had for them. He makes the point that the wonderful message of the Exodus was of no value to them because they did not believe. The implication is obvious: the message to the Hebrews would be of no value to them if they did not believe.

The author includes himself in the statement, "Now we who have believed enter that rest." The author contrasts this with the oath taken by God that those who did not believe shall never enter his rest. It is concluded that those who believe can have confidence in entering the rest, while those who do not believe cannot presume on the grace of God. He has made it clear that they will never enter his rest.

The Holy Spirit Warns Against Forfeiting God's Blessing (4:3b-11)

3 Now we who have believed enter that rest, just as God has said, "So I declared on oath in my anger, 'They shall never enter my rest.'" And yet his work has been finished since the creation of the world. 4 For somewhere he has spoken about the seventh day in these words: "And on the seventh day God rested from all his work." 5 And again in the passage above he says, "They shall never enter my rest." 6 It still remains that some will enter that rest, and those who formerly had the gospel preached to them did not go in, because of their disobedience. 7 Therefore God again set a certain day, calling it Today, when a long time later he spoke through David, as was said before: "Today, if you hear his voice, do not harden your hearts." 8 For if Joshua had given them rest, God would not have spoken later about another day. 9 There remains, then, a Sabbath-rest for the people of God; 10 for anyone who enters God's rest also rests from his own work, just as God did from his. 11 ¶ Let us, therefore, make every effort to enter that rest, so that no one will fall by following their example of disobedience.

The author turns once again to his illustration of the Israelites during the Exodus. He reminds the readers of God's oath that those who did not believe would never enter his rest.

Next he gives some of the background of what that rest is like. God's rest was instituted on the seventh day of creation. Prior to sin entering the world, Adam and Eve were experiencing that rest. MacArthur describes the situation as follows:

> Adam and Eve were completely righteous when they were created. They walked and talked with God as regularly and as naturally as they walked and talked with each other. They were at rest, in its original and its fullest sense. They relied on God for everything. They had no anxieties, no worries, no pain, no frustrations, no heartaches. They did not need God's forgiveness, because they had no sin to be forgiven of. They did not need his consolation, because they were never grieved. They did not need his encouragement, because they never failed. They only needed his fellowship, because they were made for him. This was their "rest" in God. God completed his perfect work and he rested. They were his perfect work and they rested in him. (MacArthur p 101)

Obviously, the entrance of sin into the scenario changed everything. Ever since then man has not experienced that perfect rest that Adam and Eve experienced.

The Sabbath rest occurring one day in seven is symbolic of a rest that is to be entered by believers one day. The rest currently exists but the believers entry into it is yet future. Hughes, quoting from others, observes the following:

> It is noteworthy, as Bangle observes, that Moses mentions an end of each of the first six days, but not of the seventh day - or, as Herveus puts it, that all the previous days had an evening, whereas the seventh day does not have an evening. God's rest, then, is already, and has been since the creation of the world, a reality, and it is future only in relation to the consummation promised to his people, who have yet to enter into it. (Hughes p 159)

The Example of the Israelites During 40 Years in the Past

3 Now we who have believed enter that rest, just as God has said, "So I declared on oath in my anger, 'They shall never enter my rest.'" And yet his work has been finished since the creation of the world. 4 For somewhere he has spoken about the seventh day in these words: "And on the seventh day God rested from all his work." 5 And again in the passage above he says, "They shall never enter my rest."

The author of Hebrews again emphasizes that there are some that will never enter God's rest. Referring again to the Gospel, he informs his readers that some will enter God's rest but those who had the Gospel preached to them in the wilderness did not enter the rest because of their disobedience. We already know, from the closing verses of chapter three, that disobedience and unbelief are equated. Chapter three, verse eighteen, states that those who disobeyed did not enter the rest. Verse nineteen concludes they were not able to enter because of their unbelief. Failure to believe God is disobedience and results in forfeiting the rest.

The Exhortations to the Hebrews Concerning 40 Years in the Present

6 It still remains that some will enter that rest, and those who formerly had the gospel preached to them did not go in, because of their disobedience. 7 Therefore God again set a certain day, calling it Today, when a long time later he spoke through David, as was said before: "Today, if you hear his voice, do not harden your hearts." 8 For if Joshua had given them rest, God would not have spoken later about another day. 9 There remains, then, a Sabbath-rest for the people of God; 10 for anyone who enters God's rest also rests from his own work, just as God did from his. 11 ¶ Let us, therefore, make every effort to enter that rest, so that no one will fall by following their example of disobedience.

The author wants to make certain that he convinces his readers that the rest is more than entering the promised land in Joshua's day. He wants to convince them that the rest still remains. He effectively does this by returning to Psalm 95. That Psalm was written by David long after the days of Joshua. If David was still talking about a day to enter God's rest during the age of the United Kingdom, then certainly Joshua had never provided the rest.

The author concludes that the Sabbath rest for the people of God still remains and that it is a blessing. It is something to be looked forward to by those in David's day, by the first-century Hebrews, and by believers of all ages.

The author of Hebrews encourages his audience to be eager to enter that rest. The word translated "make every effort" is the Greek "spoudazo". It literally means "to use speed" (Strong p 700). It carries the connotation of eagerness as opposed to effort. The real exhortation is "let us be eager to enter the rest." This understanding fits better in the context of belief then does the idea of making every effort. The Hebrews are to be eager to believe. Their obedience is in terms of their accepting the message as opposed to performing some task.

Disbelief once again is disobedience as explained in chapter three, verses eighteen and nineteen. Such disobedience results in falling short of the rest. Stated here in verse eleven, it reiterates what was previously stated in chapter four, verse one, "Let us be careful that none of you be found to have fallen short of it."

The author of Hebrews has skillfully used the forty year wilderness wanderings to exhort the first-century Hebrews with three warnings. Do not disbelieve God's message. Do not presume on God's grace. Do not forfeit God's rest.

The Holy Spirit Warns of God's Judgment (4:12-13)

12 For the word of God is living and active. Sharper than any double-edged sword, it penetrates even to dividing soul and spirit, joints and marrow; it judges the thoughts and attitudes of the heart. 13 Nothing in all creation is hidden from God's sight. Everything is uncovered and laid bare before the eyes of him to whom we must give account.

One final warning is yet to be given. This one is more generic and talks about the ability of the word of God to judge a person's thoughts, attitudes, motives, etc.

Thoughts & Attitudes are Judged by God's Word

12 For the word of God is living and active. Sharper than any double-edged sword, it penetrates even to dividing soul and spirit, joints and marrow; it judges the thoughts and attitudes of the heart.

In its context, the word of God spoken of here is the message given to the Israelites in the wilderness and the message given to the Hebrews in the first-century. The modern reader's mind immediately jumps to the Bible. While that is a suitable application, the context demands that it be viewed as any word given by God. The word is living and active. It was alive during the Exodus; it was alive when David wrote the Psalm, it was alive when the book of Hebrews was written, and the Bible makes it alive today.

The word is sharper than a double-edged sword. In the book of Revelation, John describes his vision of Jesus. Included in that description he says, "Out of his mouth came a sharp double edged sword." Typically, what comes out of one's mouth is words. The double-edged sword is the word of God.

The choice of a double-edged sword as the image probably resulted from the Roman soldier's prevalence in the first-century. There was a constant fear of Roman persecution and the sword. The Lord's sword is sharper than any other sword. The text says that it divides soul and spirit, bone and marrow. The implication here is not that it separates the soul and spirit, or separates the bone and marrow, but rather that it exposes them. If a sword cut through a bone it would expose the bone and the marrow. Likewise, when God's word cuts through soul and spirit it exposes what's inside.

Such exposure leads to the judgment of thoughts and attitudes. God's word is able to determine whether the

Hebrews truly believe the message or not. Jesus spoke of this as recorded in John 12:

> There is a judge for the one who rejects me and does not accept my words; that very word which I spoke will condemn him at the last day. (John 12:48)

When the time of judgment comes, it will be the words spoken by the Lord, through his prophets and apostles, and through his completed Scriptures, that will be the judge.

All Creation will be Judged by God

13 Nothing in all creation is hidden from God's sight. Everything is uncovered and laid bare before the eyes of him to whom we must give account.

The author concludes this section with the reminder that nothing is hidden from God. Someday, an account will have to be given and everything will be laid bare before the eyes of God. This final warning is designed to give the Hebrews one more reason to put their belief in God's plan and the Messiah who has come, namely, Jesus.

At the beginning of chapter three, the author urged the Hebrews to consider the apostle and high priest of their confession. The apostle is a reference to the prophet like unto Moses who was to come. Throughout chapter three and into chapter four, the author has examined Jesus by comparing the situation in the first-century to the situation in the days of Moses. The logical conclusion is that Jesus is the prophet, like unto Moses, who was to come.

The author will next turn his attention to considering the high priest of our confession.

Chapter Eight

Jesus is a High Priest Receiving a Superior Appointment (4:14 to 5:10)

He has Better Qualifications than Aaronic Priests (4:14-16)

14 Therefore, since we have a great high priest who has gone through the heavens, Jesus the Son of God, let us hold firmly to the faith we profess. 15 For we do not have a high priest who is unable to sympathize with our weaknesses, but we have one who has been tempted in every way, just as we are—yet was without sin. 16 Let us then approach the throne of grace with confidence, so that we may receive mercy and find grace to help us in our time of need.

At the beginning of chapter three, the writer exhorted his Hebrew audience to consider the apostle and high priest of our confession. He then proceeded to show that Jesus was the apostle of their confession. Jesus was indeed the one who was sent, the prophet like unto Moses.

Next the author moves to the second part of their confession, that is, the high priest. He begins by telling the Hebrews that they have a great high priest who has gone through the heavens. His name is Jesus the Son of God. The exhortation is, "Let us hold firmly to the faith we possess." The author includes himself in their profession. The faith that they professed was that they believed God's plan for a coming Messiah who would be a high priest.

As the Hebrew audience considered whether Jesus was the one who was to come, they would come to a point of decision. To reject Jesus as the planned Messiah would be to abandon their faith in God's plan. To believe that Jesus was the one who was to come would be to hold firmly to their faith. There was a life-or-death decision to be made by the Hebrews.

Jesus' Qualifications

14 Therefore, since we have a great high priest who has gone through the heavens, Jesus the Son of God, let us hold firmly to the faith we profess. 15 For we do not have a high priest who is unable to sympathize with our weaknesses, but we have one who has been tempted in every way, just as we are—yet was without sin.

The Hebrews confessed that there will be a high priest forever. The author now demonstrates that Jesus has the qualifications to be that priest. He returns to the discussion that he was engaged in just before talking about Moses. This is at the end of chapter two.

Jesus has gone through the heavens. The evidence of this truth is the death and resurrection of Jesus. This was a well-established fact during the first century. The author made reference to it in chapter two:

> But we see Jesus, who was made a little lower than the angels, now crowned with glory and honor because he suffered death, so that by the grace of God he might taste death for everyone. (Heb 2:9)

Jesus, who tasted death, was also resurrected. He was also seen ascending into heaven. All these are facts for which eyewitnesses were readily available.

Jesus is also a high priest who can sympathize with

weaknesses. This also had been discussed in chapter two:

> Since the children have flesh and blood, he
> too shared in their humanity so that by his
> death he might destroy him who holds the
> power of death—that is, the devil—and free
> those who all their lives were held in slavery
> by their fear of death. For surely it is not
> angels he helps, but Abraham's descendants.
> For this reason he had to be made like his
> brothers in every way, in order that he might
> become a merciful and faithful high priest in
> service to God, and that he might make atone-
> ment for the sins of the people. (Heb 2:14-17)

Jesus was able to sympathize because he shared their humanity, he understood their fear of death, and he made atonement for their sins.

Jesus was tempted in every way yet was without sin. This too had been discussed in chapter two:

> Because he himself suffered when he was
> tempted, he is able to help those who are
> being tempted. (Heb 2:18)

Jesus proved himself more qualified than any other priest. He had been tempted but did not succumb to those temptations. He needed no sacrifice for himself, rather made himself the sacrifice for sinful man.

Mankind's Benefits

16 Let us then approach the throne of grace with confidence, so that we may receive mercy and find grace to help us in our time of need.

125

The Hebrews who were operating under the old covenant would, of necessity, have to put confidence in their high priest. He was the one who had to approach God on their behalf. The high priest brought sacrifices before God on the Day of Atonement, and the people rejoiced when those sacrifices were accepted.

The author has presented Jesus as a great high priest. It follows that he would now invite his readers to have confidence to approach God because such a high priest exists. This verse is an invitation for them to come before the throne to receive mercy and grace.

This is an invitation to be saved. Salvation involves believing that Jesus is the one who has made atonement for mankind's sin and is the one able to restore mankind's relationship with God. They were invited to approach God because of Jesus. If the Hebrews responded to this invitation they would receive mercy and grace. Mercy involves God's withholding of the punishment that they deserved. Grace, on the other hand, is the undeserved riches of God and Christ's enablement to please God.

The phrase "In our time of need" is sometimes viewed as any time we need something from God. This does not fit the context. In the previous chapter there was a clear emphasis on "today." The exhortation was, "Today if you hear his voice do not harden your hearts..." Previously, the author had made it clear that salvation was the issue and that "today" was the time to respond to God's voice (Heb 3:7f). The "today" of chapter three and the "time of need" of chapter four are the same. The Hebrews were invited to approach the throne of grace "today."

He has a Better Calling
than Aaronic High Priests   (5:1-10)

1 ¶ Every high priest is selected from among men and is appointed to represent them in matters related to God, to offer gifts and sacrifices for sins. 2 He is able to deal gently with those who are ignorant and are going astray, since he himself is subject to weakness. 3 This is why he has to offer sacrifices for his own sins, as well as for the sins of the people. 4 No-one takes this honor upon himself; he must be called by God, just as Aaron was. 5 So Christ also did not take upon himself the glory of becoming a high priest. But God said to him, "You are my Son; today I have become your Father." 6 And he says in another place, "You are a priest forever, in the order of Melchizedek." 7 During the days of Jesus' life on earth, he offered up prayers and petitions with loud cries and tears to the one who could save him from death, and he was heard because of his reverent submission. 8 Although he was a son, he learned obedience from what he suffered 9 and, once made perfect, he became the source of eternal salvation for all who obey him 10 ¶ and was designated by God to be high priest in the order of Melchizedek.

The decision to believe that Jesus was the high priest was not easy for the Hebrews. They had been properly taught that priests had to come from the line of Aaron. It was known that Jesus was from the tribe of Judah and therefore would never be called to the priesthood.

The author must show that Jesus was called to the priesthood and that his calling is both legitimate and superior to that of Aaronic priests. He presents his arguments by first reviewing the requirements for appointment of a priest from Aaron's line. Next, utilizing Old Testament texts, he shows that the Messiah was to be from a different line of priests. Lastly, he shows that Jesus fits the requirements of the

Messiah who was to come.

Aaron's Appointment

1 ¶ Every high priest is selected from among men and is appointed to represent them in matters related to God, to offer gifts and sacrifices for sins. 2 He is able to deal gently with those who are ignorant and are going astray, since he himself is subject to weakness. 3 This is why he has to offer sacrifices for his own sins, as well as for the sins of the people. 4 No one takes this honor upon himself; he must be called by God, just as Aaron was.

The high priest's role was to be a mediator between God and man. He had to be selected from among men. Only a fellow human being would be able to deal gently with those who were ignorant and going astray. Even Jesus, to qualify as a priest, would have to be a man.

The priest was appointed to represent mankind in matters related to God. In order to do this he had to be appointed by God. Aaron's appointment is recorded in Exodus 28:

> Have Aaron your brother brought to you from among the Israelites, with his sons Nadab and Abihu, Eleazar and Ithamar, so that they may serve me as priests. (Ex 28:1)

All priests that came after Aaron would be his sons and their descendants.

The requirement that a priest be a man brought with it a difficulty. Men were sinful and no one was qualified to approach God. This is why they needed sacrifices for their own sin before they could sacrifice for the sins of others.

When considering Jesus, the Hebrews would have noted

two things about his call to the priesthood. First, he was not a descendant of Aaron and therefore could not be called. Second, he never served in the temple during his ministry. The author now has to prove that the Messiah was a priest from a different line.

The Messiah's Appointment

5 So Christ also did not take upon himself the glory of becoming a high priest. But God said to him, "You are my Son; today I have become your Father." 6 And he says in another place, "You are a priest forever, in the order of Melchizedek."

The author turns to two Messianic Psalms to demonstrate that the Christ (the Messiah) was to be a son and a high priest from a different priestly order. Once again he applies Psalm 2 to the Messiah. Jesus has always existed but at the time of the incarnation he became a man and the only begotten Son of the Father. As previously discussed, this verse also deals with his resurrection at which time he became the first-born from the dead. It is likely that the author has the incarnation in view at this time. This would prove the point that Jesus became a man and therefore could be called to be a high priest.

The other Messianic Psalm is the 110th, in which the Messiah is depicted as King:

> The LORD says to my Lord: "Sit at my right hand until I make your enemies a footstool for your feet." The LORD will extend your mighty sceptre from Zion; you will rule in the midst of your enemies. Your troops will be willing on your day of battle. Arrayed in holy majesty, from the womb of the dawn you will receive the dew of your

youth. (Psalm 110:1-3)

It is known from Jacob's blessing of his children in Genesis 50 that the Messianic king would come from the line of Judah. Jesus is from the line of Judah.

The real impact of this Psalm, in the argument of Hebrews, comes in the fourth verse:

> The LORD has sworn and will not change his mind: "You are a priest forever, in the order of Melchizedek." (Psalm 110:4)

Here it is identified that the Messianic king would also be a high priest. He would be a high priest from a different order than that of Aaron. He would be appointed by God in the order of Melchizedek.

The author will have much more to say about Melchizedek in Hebrews chapter seven; therefore, we will delay getting into the details until then. Suffice it to say that, on the basis of Psalm 110, the author of Hebrews has proven the point that the Messianic priest would be from a different line than that of Aaron.

Jesus' Appointment

7 During the days of Jesus' life on earth, he offered up prayers and petitions with loud cries and tears to the one who could save him from death, and he was heard because of his reverent submission. 8 Although he was a son, he learned obedience from what he suffered 9 and, once made perfect, he became the source of eternal salvation for all who obey him 10 ¶ and was designated by God to be high priest in the order of Melchizedek.

Having demonstrated the requirements for the Messianic priest, the author now examines Jesus and presents his qualifications for appointment to the high priest's position.

He demonstrates that he was selected from among mankind. He mentions Jesus' life on earth, as well as his offering of prayers and his obvious concern about his upcoming death. This demonstrates his ability to be sympathetic to the weaknesses of mankind.

The text could give the impression that Jesus prayed that he would not have to die. This is not the case. The participle used in the expression "save him from death" is the Greek word "ek." This word means "out from." In other words, Jesus was not praying to avoid death, rather that he would come "out from" death. This is consistent with what follows. The text said he was heard because of his reverent submission. In other words, his prayer was answered.

If Jesus' prayer had been to avoid death he did not get the answer he desired. On the other hand, if Jesus' prayer was that he come out from death, then the resurrection was the answer.

In becoming a man, Jesus also had to learn obedience. Prior to the incarnation, Jesus never had to obey anyone. When he became a son he had to obey the father:

> The one who sent me is with me; he has not
> left me alone, for I always do what pleases
> him. (John 8:29)

The concept of learning obedience carries with it the idea of learning through experience rather than simply through academic knowledge.

Likewise, in becoming a man, Jesus also suffered. Jesus was made perfect through suffering only in the sense that he became able to sympathize with mankind. There is nothing imperfect about Jesus. He did, however, have to suffer in order to have experienced all that mankind experiences. As a result of his suffering, he is now a high priest able to sympathize with mankind's weaknesses.

The high priest was also the one who brought sacrifices before God. Jesus sacrificed himself on behalf of mankind. He became the source not only of salvation but of eternal salvation for all who obey him. Once again, the idea of obedience is to believe. Several times previously the writer has used the word obedience to imply belief in God's promises.

The author draws the conclusion that Jesus was selected from among mankind; he was sympathetic to the weakness of mankind; he was sacrificed on behalf of mankind; he is the son of God; and he was saved out from death. Therefore, God appointed him to be high priest in the order of Melchizedek. The author has proved his claim that Jesus' calling to the priesthood is legitimate. The author's full discussion of Melchizedek appears in Hebrews, chapter seven.

Chapter Nine

Jesus is a High Priest Bringing Superior Teaching   (5:11 to 6:11)

Hebrews must Learn Elementary Truths Of God's Word   (5:11-14)

11 We have much to say about this, but it is hard to explain because you are slow to learn. 12 In fact, though by this time you ought to be teachers, you need someone to teach you the elementary truths of God's word all over again. You need milk, not solid food! 13 Anyone who lives on milk, being still an infant, is not acquainted with the teaching about righteousness. 14 But solid food is for the mature, who by constant use have trained themselves to distinguish good from evil.

During the first century, most of the emphasis on the coming Messiah was on his kingship. The people were looking for a political leader to overthrow Rome and usher in the kingdom age. Although there were clear prophecies about the Messiah being a high priest, they were certainly not the emphases of the Hebrews at that time. The author has briefly introduced the topic of Melchizedek. He next comments "We have much to say about this but it is hard to explain because you are slow to learn." In this statement the word "this" refers to the Melchizedekan priesthood of the Messiah.

Since that is so, the author is first going to discuss elementary teachings versus maturity, and then he will get back to the subject of Melchizedek.

Milk for the Infant

11 We have much to say about this, but it is hard to explain because you are slow to learn. 12 In fact, though by this time you ought to be teachers, you need someone to teach you the elementary truths of God's word all over again. You need milk, not solid food!

The author does not say that he will not explain the concepts to the Hebrews, rather that it is hard to explain. In the chapters that follow he will spend a good deal of time explaining about Melchizedek.

The reason given for the difficulty in explanation is that the Hebrews are slow to learn. This phrase is from a Greek word that means "limbs are numb." It implies dullness. The verb is in the past perfect tense which indicates that the dullness began in the past but has had a continuing effect up to the time of writing. This would imply that the readers were not always dull. There was a time when they were sharp enough to put their faith in Yahweh and his promise of a coming Messiah. Over time, they have become dull and are not as quick to pick up the concepts being presented to them.

The author suggests that repeated teaching is needed. He suggests that they need someone to teach them the elementary truths all over again. The word translated "elementary" is the Greek word "arche." The word means "beginning." It is the word from which we get the English word "archaic" meaning "something from long ago" or "in the beginning."

The obvious question is, "What are the beginning truths of God's word?" The answer is the Old Testament. Before the Hebrews can understand the new concepts being presented by the author, they need to understand the Old Testament teachings. He wants to present them with solid food, that is New Testament teaching, but they are still infants who need milk, that is Old Testament instruction.

Solid Food for the Mature

13 Anyone who lives on milk, being still an infant, is not acquainted with the teaching about righteousness. 14 But solid food is for the mature, who by constant use have trained themselves to distinguish good from evil.

The beginning truths of God's word are the teachings of the Old Testament which have been characterized by the author as milk. Therefore, the infants mentioned here are those Hebrew believers who are living on the Old Testament (old covenant) alone. To put that concept in the terms used by Paul in writing to the Galatians, they are children under the law, subject to guardians and trustees until the time set by the father. In Galatians, Paul contrasts the old covenant (that is the law) with the new covenant that is in Christ's blood and comes by faith. He says:

> Before this faith came, we were held prisoners by the law, locked up until faith should be revealed. So the law was put in charge to lead us to Christ that we might be justified by faith. Now that faith has come, we are no longer under the supervision of the law. You are all sons of God through faith in Christ Jesus. (Galatians 3:23-26)

Paul characterized the law as a tutor (supervisor) to bring an individual to Christ. In the Roman system in place in Paul's day, tutors were used to train young children until about the age of 13 to 16. At that time they were considered mature enough to go through a ceremony of adoption into the father's household. The author of Hebrews is using a similar analogy to suggest that these infants who are still depending on the old covenant should now be mature

135

enough to move into the new house of which Jesus Christ is the builder.

The author gives two insights into what it means to be mature. The first is that a mature person would be acquainted with the teachings about righteousness. In Jesus' day, perhaps the most revered people concerning righteousness were the Pharisees. This kind of righteousness is not what the author is speaking of. In confronting Pharisaical righteousness, Jesus said the following:

> For I tell you that unless your righteousness surpasses that of the Pharisees and the teachers of the law, you will certainly not enter the kingdom of heaven. (Matthew 5:20)

The Hebrews were acquainted with the law and thought they were acquainted with righteousness. What they needed to know, however, were the teachings of Romans 3:

> Therefore no one will be declared righteous in his sight by observing the law; rather, through the law we become conscious of sin. But now a righteousness from God, apart from law, has been made known, to which the Law and the Prophets testify. This righteousness from God comes through faith in Jesus Christ to all who believe. There is no difference (Romans 3:20-22).

Certainly the righteousness that comes through faith in Christ surpasses the righteousness of the Pharisees.

The second sign of maturity given by the author deals with distinguishing good from evil. Once again, the Old Testament believers would have pointed to the law. What could more clearly identify good and evil than the principles of the old covenant? The answer is the new covenant. In chapter eight the author quotes from Jeremiah 31:

> This is the covenant I will make with the house of Israel after that time, declares the Lord. I will put my laws in their minds and write them on their hearts. I will be their God, and they will be my people. (Heb 8:10)

The new covenant eliminates the external law in favor of an internal law. This is part of what Jesus was teaching in the Sermon on the Mount:

> You have heard that it was said, 'Do not commit adultery.' But I tell you that anyone who looks at a woman lustfully has already committed adultery with her in his heart. (Matt 5:27-28)

The old covenant law, being external, could prosecute adultery using witnesses, and impose the death penalty. The new covenant, written on the heart by the Holy Spirit, would go deeper and discern the source of the adultery which is lust.

Another example from the Sermon on the Mount deals with murder:

> "You have heard that it was said to the people long ago, 'Do not murder, and anyone who murders will be subject to judgment.' But I tell you that anyone who is angry with his brother will be subject to judgment. Again, anyone who says to his brother, 'Raca,' is answerable to the Sanhedrin. But anyone who says, 'You fool!' will be in

danger of the fire of hell." (Matt 5:21-22)

Once again, Jesus draws the distinction between the external law that prohibited murder from the internal law which judges even hatred.

This ability to evaluate internally comes from the indwelling Holy Spirit who is in all who have put their faith in Jesus Christ. Hebrews under the old covenant had their faith in a Messiah who was to come. They were infants unfamiliar with righteousness and discerning good from evil. Once they were convinced to believe that Jesus Christ was the Messiah who was to come, they would be filled with the Holy Spirit and no longer be infants but those who are mature, understanding the way of righteousness, and, with the Spirit's help, discerning good from evil internally.

This work of the Holy Spirit requires cooperation by the believer. This is why the author states that they have trained themselves to distinguish good from evil.

Hebrews must Leave Elementary Truths about the Messiah (6:1-3)

1 ¶ Therefore let us leave the elementary teachings about Christ and go on to maturity, not laying again the foundation of repentance from acts that lead to death, and of faith in God, 2 instruction about baptisms, the laying on of hands, the resurrection of the dead, and eternal judgment. 3 And God permitting, we will do so.

Elementary or beginning truths about the Messiah are those teachings that were found in the Old Testament. The Hebrews who were looking for the coming of the Messiah understood these truths and believed them. There was nothing wrong with those truths, but the author tells them it is time to leave them behind. They are to depart totally from them in order to move on to maturity.

Elementary Truths Identified

1 ¶ Therefore let us leave the elementary teachings about Christ and go on to maturity, not laying again the foundation of repentance from acts that lead to death, and of faith in God, 2 instruction about baptisms, the laying on of hands, the resurrection of the dead, and eternal judgment.

The Greek translated "elementary teachings" is "archelogon." It literally means "beginning word." If there was a beginning word, there would be more to come. The Hebrews must "go on to maturity." The word translated "go on" is from the Greek "phero" which means to be carried along. The particular construction here to be translated "let us be carried along." This word is used by Peter in describing the process of inspiration:

> For prophecy never had its origin in the will of man, but men spoke from God as they were carried along (phero) by the Holy Spirit. (2 Peter 1:21)

It is also used by Luke to describe Paul's shipwreck:

> The ship was caught by the storm and could not head into the wind; so we gave way to it and were driven along (phero). (Acts 27:15)

In Peter's writing the spirit is carrying the men along, while in Luke's the wind is carrying them along. In both cases it is a force other than themselves that they are allowing to take control. That is the emphasis here—the Hebrews

139

should allow God, through His Holy Spirit, to bring them to maturity.

At this point several of the elementary teachings, that is old covenant teachings, are identified.

The first teaching to be left is that of repentance from acts that lead to death. The concept of repentance, or turning from sin, was a predominant Old Testament teaching. Just prior to Jesus ministry his forerunner, John the Baptist, preached a message of repentance. Once Jesus went to the cross, John's message was obsolete. Clear evidence of this is given in Luke's account of Paul's encounter with some individuals at Ephesus:

> While Apollos was at Corinth, Paul took the road through the interior and arrived at Ephesus. There he found some disciples and asked them, "Did you receive the Holy Spirit when you believed?" They answered, "No, we have not even heard that there is a Holy Spirit." So Paul asked, "Then what baptism did you receive?" "John's baptism," they replied. Paul said, "John's baptism was a baptism of repentance. He told the people to believe in the one coming after him, that is, in Jesus." On hearing this, they were baptized into the name of the Lord Jesus. (Acts 19:1-5)

You will notice that John was preaching repentance and telling the people to believe in the one coming after him. This is what these individuals at Ephesus had placed their faith in. Paul now proclaims to them that the one of which John spoke was Jesus. They should believe in him and then they would receive the Holy Spirit. Their previous old covenant belief was not sufficient. They had to receive Jesus and his Holy Spirit.

The second elementary teaching dealt with faith in God. Certainly faith in God was the prevalent theme of the entire Old Testament. Having faith in God and his promises was nonetheless an elementary or beginning teaching. Their faith had to move on to make Jesus their Lord. When leaving Ephesus Paul made that point clear:

> I have declared to both Jews and Greeks that
> they must turn to God in repentance and have
> faith in our Lord Jesus. (Acts 20:21)

Without faith in the Lord Jesus, they cannot be saved. Once again this is consistent with Jesus' teaching. He said in the upper room:

> Jesus answered, "I am the way and the truth
> and the life. No one comes to the Father
> except through me. (John 14:6)

Faith in God and his promise of the Messiah is no longer sufficient. Faith must be in Jesus, the Messiah who has come.

> Do not let your hearts be troubled. You trust
> in God; trust also in me. (John 14:1)

The third elementary truth dealt with instructions about baptisms. The word translated baptisms is translated differently in chapter nine, verse ten:

> They are only a matter of food and drink and
> various ceremonial washings—external regu-
> lations applying until the time of the new
> order. (Heb 9:10)

The word is translated "ceremonial washings." In the immediate context of chapter nine, it is contrasting the activities of the old covenant to the activities of the new covenant. Ceremonial washings was one of the old covenant activities. The verses we are dealing with in chapter six are also contrasting Old Testament activities with New Testament teachings. It is therefore appropriate, and even compelling, to translate the word as "ceremonial washings."

No longer do the Hebrews have to deal with the ceremonial washings of the Law. Instead, they are to move on to the teachings Paul gave to Titus:

> But when the kindness and love of God our Savior appeared, he saved us, not because of righteous things we had done, but because of his mercy. He saved us through the washing of rebirth and renewal by the Holy Spirit, whom he poured out on us generously through Jesus Christ our Savior, so that, having been justified by his grace, we might become heirs having the hope of eternal life. (Titus 3:4-7)

The ceremonial washings were a "type" of what was to come. Jesus is the "antitype," or fulfillment, of those elementary teachings.

The next teaching to be abandoned deals with the laying on of hands. The Hebrews, who were faithfully involved in temple worship and sacrifice, would have understood the laying on of hands as the teaching of Leviticus, chapter one:

> If the offering is a burnt offering from the herd, he is to offer a male without defect. He must present it at the entrance to the Tent of Meeting so that it will be acceptable to the

> LORD. He is to lay his hand on the head of
> the burnt offering, and it will be accepted on
> his behalf to make atonement for him. He is
> to slaughter the young bull before the
> LORD, and then Aaron's sons the priests
> shall bring the blood and sprinkle it against
> the altar on all sides at the entrance to the
> Tent of Meeting. (Lev 1:3-5)

Whenever an animal was to be sacrificed, the individual bringing the sacrifice would lay his hand on the head of the animal and confess his sin. He was thereby ceremonially transferring his sin to the sacrifice. This was a type, of which Jesus would be the fulfillment. Paul's second letter to the Corinthians describes this transfer of a believer's sin to the Lord Jesus:

> God made him who had no sin to be sin for
> us, so that in him we might become the righ-
> teousness of God. (2 Cor 5:21)

The sacrificial system and the laying on of hands was the type but the reality is found in Christ. The type must be abandoned by the Hebrews in favor of the Messiah who has come and sacrificed his life on their behalf, that is, Jesus.

The next elementary truth deals with the resurrection of the dead. The Old Testament believer understood that there would be a resurrection at the last day. They did not have the full picture, however, until Jesus came. When Lazarus of Bethany died, Jesus told his sister Martha that her brother would rise. The encounter went as follows:

> Jesus said to her, "Your brother will rise
> again." Martha answered, "I know he will
> rise again in the resurrection at the last day."

> Jesus said to her, "I am the resurrection and the life. He who believes in me will live, even though he dies; and whoever lives and believes in me will never die. Do you believe this?" "Yes, Lord," she told him, "I believe that you are the Christ, the Son of God, who was to come into the world." (John 11:23-27)

Jesus has taken the resurrection to a new level as he declares himself to be the resurrection and the life. Only those who believe in him will never die.

Notice Martha's confession of faith. She says that Jesus is the Messiah, the Son of God, who was to come into the world. Here is a clear example of someone who was looking for the coming Messiah and who has expressed her faith in Jesus as the Messiah who has come. That is what the entire book of Hebrews is about.

The next elementary teaching to leave behind deals with eternal judgment. The Old Testament contained many teachings about judgment. To be sure, the law would be that which would bring judgment upon each individual as he stood before God. Those living under the law could never fulfill its righteous requirements. Jesus, however, could. Because of Jesus, the idea of judgment has been changed. Paul, writing to the Romans, concludes:

> Therefore, there is now no condemnation for those who are in Christ Jesus, because through Christ Jesus the law of the Spirit of life set me free from the law of sin and death. For what the law was powerless to do in that it was weakened by the sinful nature, God did by sending his own Son in the likeness of sinful man to be a sin offering. And so he condemned sin in sinful man, in order that

the righteous requirements of the law might
be fully met in us, who do not live according
to the sinful nature but according to the
Spirit. (Rom 8:1-4)

Punishment has been dealt out at the cross and therefore
there is no condemnation for those who are in Christ.
Eternal judgment was a tutor to bring individuals to see their
need for Christ. Now that Jesus, the Messiah has come, true
believers put their security in him and have no fear of eternal judgment. All of the sacrificial system and old covenant
teachings were types of which Christ is the reality.

God's Sovereign Control

3 And God permitting, we will do so.

Jesus taught the disciples on the road to Emmaus that he
was the fulfillment of those things written in the Old
Testament:

He said to them, "This is what I told you
while I was still with you: Everything must
be fulfilled that is written about me in the
law of Moses, the Prophets and the Psalm."
Then he opened their minds so they could
understand the Scriptures. (Luke 24:44-45)

Notice that Jesus not only gave them information but
also opened their minds so that they could understand. The
writer of Hebrews was aware that his explaining the truth of
the Messiah would not be sufficient to bring people to maturity. He was aware that they would only come to understanding and belief through the sovereign control of God.
While he urges them to go on to maturity, he adds the provi-

sion, "And God permitting, we will do so." Unless God opens their minds they will not understand.

Hebrews must Understand the Results of Rejecting God's Son   (6:4-8)

4 It is impossible for those who have once been enlightened, who have tasted the heavenly gift, who have shared in the Holy Spirit, 5 who have tasted the goodness of the word of God and the powers of the coming age, 6 if they fall away, to be brought back to repentance, because to their loss they are crucifying the Son of God all over again and subjecting him to public disgrace. 7 Land that drinks in the rain often falling on it and that produces a crop useful to those for whom it is farmed receives the blessing of God. 8 But land that produces thorns and thistles is worthless and is in danger of being cursed. In the end it will be burned.

The exhortations continue for the Hebrews to go on to maturity by receiving the Messiah that has come. The author next gives a stern warning. Its purpose is to allow the Hebrews to understand clearly the results of rejecting God's Son. He describes their current situation and then what will happen if they do not respond to what they know.

Results of Rejecting

4 It is impossible for those who have once been enlightened, who have tasted the heavenly gift, who have shared in the Holy Spirit, 5 who have tasted the goodness of the word of God and the powers of the coming age, 6 if they fall away, to be brought back to repentance, because to their loss they are crucifying the Son of God all over again and subjecting him to public disgrace.

Five expressions are used to identify the spiritual condition of the audience. All of these expressions deal with someone who is saved under the old covenant with faith in the coming Messiah. First, they have been enlightened. This does not imply conversion but rather being exposed to the light. The prophet Isaiah, in speaking of the Messiah, referred to him as being a great light. Isaiah, chapter nine, verses one and two, are quoted in the book of Matthew:

> When Jesus heard that John had been put in prison, he returned to Galilee. Leaving Nazareth, he went and lived in Capernaum, which was by the lake in the area of Zebulun and Naphtali—to fulfill what was said through the prophet Isaiah: "Land of Zebulun and land of Naphtali, the way to the sea, along the Jordan, Galilee of the Gentiles—the people living in darkness have seen a great light; on those living in the land of the shadow of death a light has dawned." (Matt 4:12-16)

Even if the Hebrews had not personally been exposed to Jesus, they are now hearing about him through the letter to the Hebrews. They, in that sense, have been exposed to the light.

Second, they have tasted the heavenly gift. The heavenly gift is the gift of faith. Ephesians 2 says, "By grace you have been saved through faith-and that not of yourself-it is the gift of God." (Eph 2:8-9) The faith that the Hebrews had was Old Testament faith in a coming Messiah. There faith certainly was a gift from God. It would have to go a step further however, now that Jesus was here.

Third, they shared in the Holy Spirit. The word "shared" is the same word translated "companions" in Hebrews 1:9.

It implies association with but not possession of. The Hebrews had certainly experienced the work of the Holy Spirit but they were not indwelt by the Holy Spirit as New Testament saints are.

Fourth, they have tasted the goodness of the word of God. The term used for "word" is "rhema" not "logos." This makes is clear that they have received portions of the written word but this is not a reference to the living word. In Romans, chapter nine, Paul, speaking of Israelites who were cut off, nonetheless describes them as having received the covenants, the law and the promises. They have certainly tasted of the word of God which now brings them to a decision point concerning Jesus.

Fifth, they have tasted the power of the coming age. The sense in which they have tasted this power is by being eyewitnesses to miracles. They have seen healings, miracles and other manifestations of the Spirit both in the life of Jesus and in the lives of his apostles. These manifestations were for the purpose of bringing them to a saving understanding of who Jesus was.

The author now warns about falling away. To fall away means to deviate from the right path, to wander or turn aside. These Old Testament believers have been exposed to the truth. If they turn aside and defect from the pursuit of truth, there will be dire consequences.

The condition of the Hebrews, before hearing about Jesus, was one of being saved by faith in a coming Messiah. They had repented of their sin, believed the promises of God, and became old covenant saints. They demonstrated their faith by keeping the sacrificial system.

Now that these Hebrews have been exposed to Jesus, the once-for-all sacrifice for sin, they have to decide whether they will accept his sacrifice as their own. They may think that they can simply turn their back on Jesus and return to their former condition. The author of Hebrews says that is impossible. They cannot be brought back to their previous condition of repentance.

He does not just say it is difficult but that it is impossible. The Greek word translated "impossible" is the same word used in Hebrews 6:18 to say that it is impossible for God to lie. It is also used in Hebrews 10:4 to say it is impossible for the blood of bulls and goats to take away sins. There is no question that it is impossible for them to go back to their former condition.

This has always been one of the more difficult passages of Hebrews. The typical argument is whether one can lose his salvation or not. Those in the Armenian camp would use this verse to demonstrate that the Bible teaches that you can lose your salvation. Those in the Calvinistic camp would work hard to demonstrate another interpretation of the meaning of "fall away." When one properly understands the audience (Hebrews saved under the old covenant), one realizes that this is a unique situation during a unique time frame.

Those saved under the old covenant, alive at this time, must make a decision about the Messianic claim of Jesus. If they reject Jesus they cannot be saved. Their old covenant salvation worked for them until Jesus arrived but they will lose their salvation if they do not receive him as Savior. No other generation on earth has ever been in this unique situation.

If, after examining the facts about Jesus, the Hebrews turned aside and did not receive him, they would be declaring him a false prophet. In so doing they would be agreeing that his crucifixion was appropriate. If Jesus was not who he said he was, then he was a false prophet who deserves to be killed. If the Hebrews decide not to receive Jesus then they are crucifying the Son of God again and subjecting him to public disgrace.

An Illustration of Contrasting Results

7 Land that drinks in the rain often falling on it and that produces a crop useful to those for whom it is farmed receives the blessing of God. 8 But land that produces thorns and thistles is worthless and is in danger of being cursed. In the end it will be burned.

A stern warning has been delivered and the dire consequences described. The author next presents an illustration of good land and bad land. One receives blessing while the other receives cursing. This is illustrative of the two covenants that have been discussed. The old covenant, that is, the law, brings a curse. Paul speaks of that to the church of Galatia:

> Christ redeemed us from the curse of the law
> by becoming a curse for us, for it is written:
> "Cursed is everyone who is hung on a tree."
> (Gal 3:13)

Not only does Paul refer to the curse of the law, but in the same verse he demonstrates its remedy, that is, Christ. Jesus spoke of the new covenant as being in his blood. He is the remedy for the curse of the law. He supplies the blessing of the new covenant.

At this point in history, the old covenant was obsolete and about to be discarded. In 70 AD, when the temple was destroyed, all the trappings of the old covenant were gone.

Hebrews must Understand the Results of Accepting God's Son   (6:9-11)

9 ¶ Even though we speak like this, dear friends, we are confident of better things in your case—things that accompany salvation. 10 God is not unjust; he will not forget your work and the love you have shown him as you have helped his people and continue to help them. 11 We want each of you to show this same diligence to the very end, in order to make your hope sure.

The stern warning has been given, the dire consequences of rejecting Jesus have been described, an illustration of contrasting results has been given, and now the author encourages the Hebrews with words of hope.

Past Obedience Remembered

9 ¶ Even though we speak like this, dear friends, we are confident of better things in your case—things that accompany salvation. 10 God is not unjust; he will not forget your work and the love you have shown him as you have helped his people and continue to help them.

The author gave his audience a stern warning; however, he anticipated a positive result to come from his urging. The Hebrews had been on their way to paradise through their faith in God's promised Messiah. The author is confident that many, if not all of them, will now believe in Jesus. This was the urging done by Jesus in the upper room when he said, "You believe in God, believe also in Me." (John 14:1) The author is expressing confidence that the Hebrews will make the right decision.

Assuming they make the right decision, here is what happens. God will not forget their work. The work to this point was belief in and obedience to the old covenant. In Matthew 22, Jesus summed up the old covenant law in two commandments:

Jesus replied: "'Love the Lord your God

with all your heart and with all your soul and with all your mind.' This is the first and greatest commandment. And the second is like it: 'Love your neighbor as yourself.' All the law and the Prophets hang on these two commandments." (Matt 22:37-40)

Loving God and loving others are what the law and prophets were all about. The writer to Hebrews says that their love for God and help for his people will not be forgotten. When a Hebrew believer in the old covenant turns his faith to Jesus, his past obedience will be remembered as well.

Future Obedience Continues

11 We want each of you to show this same diligence to the very end, in order to make your hope sure.

The Hebrews demonstrated great diligence in their belief in and obedience to the old covenant. It was not easy to be a practicing Jew under the Roman occupation but they remained strong in their faith. Having been diligent in the past, the author urges them to continue in their diligence. This would require them to receive Jesus as Savior which would in turn make their hope of eternal life sure.

Chapter Ten

Jesus is a High Priest Providing
Superior Hope   (6:12 to 6:20)

There is a Promise
to be Inherited   (6:12-15)

12 We do not want you to become lazy, but to imitate those who through faith and patience inherit what has been promised. 13 When God made his promise to Abraham, since there was no one greater for him to swear by, he swore by himself, 14 saying, "I will surely bless you and give you many descendants." 15 And so after waiting patiently, Abraham received what was promised.

The last section ended with the author desiring that the Hebrews would show diligence and make their hope sure. He now turns his attention to Jesus, the one who provides a superior hope. Their hope could not be sure unless it was in Jesus.

He takes his readers back beyond the law to the promises given to Abraham. He wants to remind them that there has always been a promise to be inherited that was apart from the law.

Inherited by Faith

12 We do not want you to become lazy, but to imitate those who through faith and patience inherit what has been promised.

We do not want you to become lazy. The word "lazy" is the same word translated in chapter five, verse eleven, as "slow to learn". Here, as there, it has the idea of being "dull." Lazy usually has the idea of failure to do work. That is not what is in view here. Instead, it is failure to grasp the truth.

The author wants his readers to imitate Abraham. The two characteristics of Abraham to be imitated were faith and patience. Abraham believed God and he credited it to him as righteousness (Gen 15:6). Abraham's entire walk with the Lord was characterized by patience. When he left his homeland he was 75 years old. He did not know where the Lord was bringing him but patiently awaited instructions. Likewise, when the promise of a child was given, Abraham had to wait until he was 100 years old to see that promise fulfilled. Sometimes in the narrative it appeared that Abraham was less than patient. (Hagar/Ishmael); however, God developed patience in him over time.

Made by the Greatest

13 When God made his promise to Abraham, since there was no one greater for him to swear by, he swore by himself, 14 saying, "I will surely bless you and give you many descendants." 15 And so after waiting patiently, Abraham received what was promised.

The incident of God swearing by himself is recorded in Genesis 22. It follows the account of God testing Abraham by asking that he sacrifice his one and only son Isaac. After Isaac was spared, God again revealed himself to Abraham:

> The angel of the LORD called to Abraham
> from heaven a second time and said, "I swear
> by myself, declares the LORD, that because
> you have done this and have not withheld

your son, your only son, I will surely bless you and make your descendants as numerous as the stars in the sky and as the sand on the seashore. Your descendants will take possession of the cities of their enemies, and through your offspring all nations on earth will be blessed, because you have obeyed me." (Gen 22:15-18)

This promise includes land, seed and blessing. This is a trio of promises that was made not only to Abraham but also to his descendants. Abraham did see the partial fulfillment of those promises as his family began to grow. The real fulfillment of the promise of sons for Abraham would be realized through the person of the Messiah. Paul describes this in Galatians:

The promises were spoken to Abraham and to his seed. The Scripture does not say "and to seeds," meaning many people, but "and to your seed," meaning one person, who is Christ. (Gal 3:16)

Jesus is the seed that was spoken of. Paul continues to demonstrate the relationship of believers to both Jesus and Abraham:

You are all sons of God through faith in Christ Jesus, for all of you who were baptized into Christ have clothed yourselves with Christ. There is neither Jew nor Greek, slave nor free, male nor female, for you are all one in Christ Jesus. If you belong to Christ, then you are Abraham's seed, and heirs according to the promise. (Gal 3:26-29)

The promise to Abraham is fulfilled in the person of Jesus.

The writer of the book of Hebrews has set up Abraham's faith in the promise as an example for the Hebrews. They are to imitate the faith of Abraham and believe the promise made by God himself. God swore by himself because there is no greater. This promise is made by the greatest.

There is a Promise made with God's Oath (6:16-18)

16 Men swear by someone greater than themselves, and the oath confirms what is said and puts an end to all argument. 17 Because God wanted to make the unchanging nature of his purpose very clear to the heirs of what was promised, he confirmed it with an oath. 18 God did this so that, by two unchangeable things in which it is impossible for God to lie, we who have fled to take hold of the hope offered to us may be greatly encouraged.

Having referred his readers to the promise made to Abraham, the author of Hebrews now ensures that they understand the certainty of that promise. He describes the oath that accompanied the promise. Once he solidified their understanding of the promise, he then moves on to Jesus and how he secured the promise.

The Power of an Oath

16 Men swear by someone greater than themselves, and the oath confirms what is said and puts an end to all argument.

The very idea of an oath is to appeal to someone greater then the person making the oath. Someone might say, "I swear by my mother that I am telling the truth." In a courtroom the oath to tell the truth is taken with a hand on the Bible as being the authority greater than themselves. The oath puts an end to all arguments in the sense that it ensures the honesty and integrity of the person making the oath.

The Purpose of God's Oath

17 Because God wanted to make the unchanging nature of his purpose very clear to the heirs of what was promised, he confirmed it with an oath. 18 God did this so that, by two unchangeable things in which it is impossible for God to lie, we who have fled to take hold of the hope offered to us may be greatly encouraged.

The promise to Abraham was of such significance that God made certain that mankind understood its unchanging nature. The promise would endure from Abraham throughout the ages to the time of the writing of the book of Hebrews and, indeed, even to today. He made it clear that his promise was valid by confirming it with an oath.

The text speaks of two unchangeable things in which it is impossible for God to lie. These two unchangeable things are first, the promise of God given in Genesis 15:4-5 and second, the oath of God made in Genesis 22:15-19. It is impossible for God to lie when he is making a promise. It is also impossible for God to lie when he is proclaiming an oath. Since this is so, the hope offered by the promise is very secure. This was to be a tremendous encouragement to the Hebrews.

There is a Promise
Secured by Jesus   (6:19-20)

19 We have this hope as an anchor for the soul, firm and secure. It enters the inner sanctuary behind the curtain, 20 where Jesus, who went before us, has entered on our behalf. He has become a high priest forever, in the order of Melchizedek.

The promise of blessing made to Abraham and his descendants was presented and confirmed with an oath. The author then connects that promise to the activities of Jesus and begins dealing with his priesthood in earnest.

The Believer's Hope

19 We have this hope as an anchor for the soul, firm and secure. It enters the inner sanctuary behind the curtain, 20 where Jesus, who went before us, has entered on our behalf.

The author uses a sailing metaphor in describing the hope that has been secured by Jesus. He describes the hope as an anchor for the soul. Even though a ship might be tossed about, as long as the anchor holds, it will be safe. The anchor of hope described here is firm and secure.

The illustration then takes that anchor into the inner sanctuary behind the curtain. This reference would be well known by the Hebrew readers. It described the process of the high priest going into the temple and then behind the curtain into the Holy of Holies. The author also states that Jesus has entered on our behalf. This is not speaking of the earthly tabernacle for Jesus never entered the Holy of Holies. It is instead referring to the sanctuary in heaven. The temple on earth was just a shadow of the reality that is in heaven. Jesus, after his resurrection, ascended into heaven and is seated at the right hand of the Most High.

Believers are currently tossed to and fro in the earth realm, but the anchor chain leads up to heaven and the anchor has been firmly established in the Most Holy Place by Jesus.

Some of the harbors in the Mediterranean Sea could not

be entered by large ships during bad weather. They would stay at sea but take their anchor into the harbor. The anchor would be lowered into a small boat called the forerunner. The forerunner would carry the anchor and firmly establish it in the harbor. Jesus, the forerunner, carried the anchor of hope into heaven and established it, firm and secure.

Jesus' Priesthood

He has become a high priest forever, in the order of Melchizedek.

Once the author presents the fact that Jesus entered into the Most Holy Place, he deals with the concept of priesthood. Only a God-appointed high priest could enter into the Holy of Holies in the tabernacle. He had to show that Jesus was indeed a God-appointed high priest.

Everyone knew that Jesus was not from the tribe of Levi and a descendant of Aaron. Appealing once again to the 110th Psalm, the author makes the point that Jesus is a high priest of the order of Melchizedek. He now turns his attention to demonstrating the superiority of Jesus' priesthood to that of Aaron's.

Chapter Eleven

Jesus is a High Priest Establishing a Superior Priesthood (7:1 to 7:28)

Jesus' Priesthood is in the Order Of Melchizedek (7:1-3)

1 ¶ This Melchizedek was king of Salem and priest of God Most High. He met Abraham returning from the defeat of the kings and blessed him, 2 and Abraham gave him a tenth of everything. First, his name means "king of righteousness"; then also, "king of Salem" means "king of peace." 3 Without father or mother, without genealogy, without beginning of days or end of life, like the Son of God he remains a priest forever.

The author now turns in earnest to teaching about the Melchizedekan priesthood. He develops this doctrine utilizing only four verses from the book of Genesis and then applies it to the Messiah using one verse from the book of Psalms. Despite the brevity of the Old Testament accounts of Melchizedek, the arguments made for the Messiah being a high priest in the order of Melchizedek are compelling.

Melchizedek Meets Abraham

1 ¶ This Melchizedek was king of Salem and priest of God Most High. He met Abraham returning from the defeat of the kings and blessed him, 2 and Abraham gave him a tenth of everything.

The account of Abraham meeting Melchizedek is found

in Genesis chapter 14. Abraham was returning from a battle, having delivered his nephew Lot from capture. Lot had been taken captive by kings that had seized all the goods of Sodom and Gomorrah where Lot was living. As Abraham returned he met Melchizedek:

> After Abram returned from defeating Kedorlaomer and the kings allied with him, the king of Sodom came out to meet him in the Valley of Shaveh (that is, the King's Valley). Then Melchizedek king of Salem brought out bread and wine. He was priest of God Most High, and he blessed Abram, saying, "Blessed be Abram by God Most High, Creator of heaven and earth. And blessed be God Most High, who delivered your enemies into your hand." Then Abram gave him a tenth of everything. (Gen 14:17-20)

Melchizedek held the title of the King of Salem. This is the ancient name for Jerusalem, and this is its first mention in Scripture. There is an obvious link between this early King of Jerusalem and the ultimate King Messiah who will reign from Jerusalem.

Melchizedek is also described as a priest of God Most High. He is not described as a priest of Yahweh but rather a priest of El Elyon. This designation serves well to show a priesthood that goes beyond just Israel to the entire world. The term Yahweh would usually refer to Israel's covenant keeping God while El Elyon would broaden to the God of both Jews and Gentiles.

The concept of a priesthood for Jews and Gentiles was important to the first-century Hebrews as the church was being formed. It was an assembly of both Jews and Gentiles.

While both the old covenant and the new covenant were made with Israel, the Gentiles had been grafted into the new covenant. Some believe that the serving of bread and wine by Melchizedek is symbolic of the new covenant. Jesus spoke of the new covenant in his blood when he served bread and wine to his disciples at the Last Supper. While it is never stated in the New Testament that Melchizedek's bread and wine were a type of what was to come, the link is too obvious to go unmentioned.

Melchizedek blessed Abraham and Abraham gave him a tithe of the spoils taken from the kings. A few verses later the author of Hebrews expounds on the significance of these activities.

Likeness to the Messiah Apparent

First, his name means "king of righteousness"; then also, "king of Salem" means "king of peace." 3 Without father or mother, without genealogy, without beginning of days or end of life, like the Son of God he remains a priest forever.

Once again the author refers to the 110th Psalm, a clear Messianic Psalm. He quotes from verse four:

> The LORD has sworn and will not change
> his mind: "You are a priest forever, in the
> order of Melchizedek." (Psalm 110:4)

The point had previously been made that it was the Son of God who would fulfill this prophecy of being a priest forever. There are a few significant points made about the priesthood.

First, it is a universal priesthood. As discussed, Melchizedek was called priest of God Most High. Use of El Elyon showed the universal nature of the priesthood.

Second, it was to be a royal priesthood. Melchizedek was not only a priest but he was also a king—the king of Jerusalem. In the 110th Psalm, the Lord God not only promised that the Messiah would be a priest forever but also that he would be a king reigning from Jerusalem:

> The LORD will extend your mighty sceptre from Zion; you will rule in the midst of your enemies. (Psalm 110:2)

The mighty sceptre of the Messianic king would extend from Jerusalem.

Third, it was a priesthood of righteousness and peace. Melchizedek means king of righteousness while his title, King of Salem, means "king of peace." The only real righteousness that mankind can experience is the righteousness of Christ. Likewise, the only peace man can have with God is through Jesus, the Messiah who has come.

Fourth, it was a priesthood without Levitical genealogy. Melchizedek is described as being without father or mother, without genealogy and without beginning of days or end of life. This could be taken in a literal sense in which case the appearance of Melchizedek may have been a Christophony, that is, an Old Testament appearance of Jesus. Alternatively, it could be taken in a literary sense, in which case this description is presented in order to make him a type of Christ. In other words, Christ was in a real sense what Melchizedek was in a literary sense. In either scenario, the real point is that Melchizedek did not need a Levitical genealogy in order to be God's priest.

Fifth, it was an eternal priesthood. The priesthood of Melchizedek, fulfilled by the Son of God, would last forever.

Jesus' Priesthood
is Better than the Levitical Priesthood   (7:4-10)

4 Just think how great he was: Even the patriarch Abraham gave him a tenth of the plunder! 5 Now the law requires the descendants of Levi who become priests to collect a tenth from the people—that is, their brothers—even though their brothers are descended from Abraham. 6 This man, however, did not trace his descent from Levi, yet he collected a tenth from Abraham and blessed him who had the promises. 7 And without doubt the lesser person is blessed by the greater. 8 In the one case, the tenth is collected by men who die; but in the other case, by him who is declared to be living. 9 One might even say that Levi, who collects the tenth, paid the tenth through Abraham, 10 because when Melchizedek met Abraham, Levi was still in the body of his ancestor.

The first-century Hebrews certainly believed in the greatness of Abraham. In an encounter with the Pharisees Jesus declared himself to be greater than Abraham. John's gospel records the Pharisees question:

"... Are you greater than our father Abraham? he died, and so did the prophets. Who do you think you are?" Jesus replied, "If I glorify myself, my glory means nothing. My Father, whom you claim as your God, is the one who glorifies me. Though you do not know him, I know him. If I said I did not, I would be a liar like you, but I do know him and keep his word. Your father Abraham rejoiced at the thought of seeing my day; he saw it and was glad." "You are not yet fifty years old," the Jews said to him, "and you have seen Abraham!" "I tell you the truth,"

Jesus answered, "before Abraham was born, I am!" At this, they picked up stones to stone him, but Jesus hid himself, slipping away from the temple grounds. (John 8:53-59)

One cannot help but wonder when Abraham saw the day of Jesus. Perhaps the encounter with Melchizedek was the event where Abraham saw Jesus' day. This would be particularly true if Melchizedek was a Christophony.

The author of Hebrews now describes the importance of this encounter between Abraham and Melchizedek.

Received Tithe from Abraham

4 Just think how great he was: Even the patriarch Abraham gave him a tenth of the plunder! 5 Now the law requires the descendants of Levi who become priests to collect a tenth from the people—that is, their brothers—even though their brothers are descended from Abraham. 6 This man, however, did not trace his descent from Levi, yet he collected a tenth from Abraham and blessed him who had the promises. 7 And without doubt the lesser person is blessed by the greater. 8 In the one case, the tenth is collected by men who die; but in the other case, by him who is declared to be living.

Think how great Melchizedek was. The word translated "think" means "to consider carefully." The author draws attention to two activities that occurred in the Abraham/Melchizedek encounter - a tithe and a blessing.

At the time of Abraham, the law and the Levitical priesthood were hundreds of years in the future. When it was enacted, the law would require Israelites to tithe to the descendants of Levi who became priests. Abraham's tithe to Melchizedek was not a matter of law. He tithed because of the greatness and superiority of Melchizedek. There was something about that encounter that made it clear that Melchizedek was greater than Abraham, so Abraham willingly presented him with a tenth of all the plunder. Melchizedek collected this tithe long before Levi was even born.

Melchizedek also blessed Abraham. Abraham was considered the greatest of the patriarchs because he had the promises. The covenant promising Israel a land, seed and blessing was given to Abraham. Despite Abraham's greatness, he was a lesser person then Melchizedek. Melchizedek demonstrated that he was the greater person by blessing Abraham. Abraham demonstrated that he concurred with that evaluation by accepting the blessing and also by tithing to Melchizedek.

The point is also made that tithes to the Levitical priesthood are given to men who die. Abraham's tithe to Melchizedek was given to one who is declared to be living. This again demonstrated the eternal nature of the priesthood to be given to the Messiah.

Received Tithe from Levi

9 One might even say that Levi, who collects the tenth, paid the tenth through Abraham, 10 because when Melchizedek met Abraham, Levi was still in the body of his ancestor.

An interesting point is now made about Levi. He obviously was not alive at the time of Abraham. Abraham's son was Isaac, who's son was Jacob who was the father of twelve, one of whom was Levi. When Abraham met Melchizedek, Levi was still in the body of his ancestor. The author of Hebrews suggests that Levi paid a tithe through Abraham. Obviously, this concept could extend to Aaron as well, because he was in the body of his ancestor Levi.

The point is that Melchizedek was greater than the

Levitical priesthood. Jesus, the Messiah who has come, is a high priest of the order of Melchizedek. He too is greater than Abraham, Levi, and Aaron.

Jesus' Priesthood
is Replacing the Levitical Priesthood   (7:11-12)

11 ¶ If perfection could have been attained through the Levitical priesthood (for on the basis of it the law was given to the people), why was there still need for another priest to come—one in the order of Melchizedek, not in the order of Aaron? 12 For when there is a change of the priesthood, there must also be a change of the law.

The purpose of any priesthood is to draw men close to God and to remove the obstacle of sin which separates man from God. The Levitical priesthood failed to do this. It was destined for failure because it was a type and incomplete. It pointed to the Messiah who would be the antitype. The Levitical priesthood was only a shadow, whereas the priesthood of the Messiah would be the reality.

Failure of Levitical Priesthood

11 ¶ If perfection could have been attained through the Levitical priesthood (for on the basis of it the law was given to the people), why was there still need for another priest to come—one in the order of Melchizedek, not in the order of Aaron?

Perfection, sometimes translated maturity, literally means to bring to consummation. The author makes the point that the Levitical priesthood could never accomplish the goals of bringing men close to God and removing the obstacle of sin. He links the priesthood and law. Obviously, it is violations of the law that require the involvement of a priest.

If the Levitical priesthood was effective, why would another priesthood be needed? There are two Greek words that can be translated "another." The first is "allos". This means "another of the same kind." It is the word Jesus uses when he promises "another comforter" in John 14:16. The second word is "heteros." It means "another of a different kind." Paul uses it in Galatians when he speaks of "another gospel." It is "heteros" that is used in this Hebrews' passage which supports the fact that the Messianic priest would be "of a different kind" than the Aaronic priests.

According to the 110th Psalm, the Messiah would not be a Levitical priest but rather a priest of the order of Melchizedek. The author of Hebrews makes the point that the Levitical system must be replaced. It was never intended to last because it was only a shadow of the reality that would be found in the Messianic priesthood.

Changed Priesthood Requires Changed Law

12 For when there is a change of the priesthood, there must also be a change of the law.

Just as the Levitical priesthood was to be set aside in favor of the Messiah, so likewise the law would be set aside at the coming of the Messiah. Paul, in writing to the Galatians, made the point that the law was temporary until the Messiah came:

> What, then, was the purpose of the law? It was added because of transgressions until the Seed to whom the promise referred had come. The law was put into effect through angels by a mediator. (Gal 3:19)

Just as the Levitical priesthood could not draw men close to God and remove the obstacle of sin, neither could the law. Paul also makes that point in Galatians 3:

> Is the law, therefore, opposed to the promises of God? Absolutely not! For if a law had been given that could impart life, then righteousness would certainly have come by the law. But the Scripture declares that the whole world is a prisoner of sin, so that what was promised, being given through faith in Jesus Christ, might be given to those who believe. (Gal 3:21-22)

The law was ineffective in its ability to save an individual. The Levitical priesthood was ineffective in its ability to save a person. Salvation comes only through Jesus Christ, the Messiah who has come. The Levitical priesthood and the law were set aside in favor of the work of Jesus Christ on the cross of Calvary.

Jesus' Priesthood is Established on a Better Basis (7:13-17)

13 He of whom these things are said belonged to a different tribe, and no one from that tribe has ever served at the altar. 14 For it is clear that our Lord descended from Judah, and in regard to that tribe Moses said nothing about priests. 15 And what we have said is even more clear if another priest like Melchizedek appears, 16 one who has become a priest not on the basis of a regulation as to his ancestry but on the basis of the power of an indestructible life. 17 For it is declared: "You are a priest forever, in the order of Melchizedek."

No one could become a priest unless he was appointed

by God. There were two ways for this appointment to be made. One way was to be in the genealogy of Aaron which would qualify one to become a priest. The other way was to be a priest like Melchizedek who had no beginning of days or end of life. The text now proceeds to demonstrate that Jesus became a Melchizedekan priest through the power of an indestructible life.

Jesus from a Different Tribe

13 He of whom these things are said belonged to a different tribe, and no one from that tribe has ever served at the altar. 14 For it is clear that our Lord descended from Judah, and in regard to that tribe Moses said nothing about priests.

The first-century Hebrews knew that the Messiah would come from the tribe of Judah. Once the Messianic kingship and priesthood were linked, a problem existed. Priests did not come from the tribe of Judah. Priests came from the tribe of Levi. There was never a precedence that anyone from the tribe of Judah had served at the altar. Jesus, the Messiah who had come, was of the tribe of Judah. His priesthood would be in question unless there was a different priesthood.

Jesus a Priest like Melchizedek

15 And what we have said is even more clear if another priest like Melchizedek appears, 16 one who has become a priest not on the basis of a regulation as to his ancestry but on the basis of the power of an indestructible life. 17 For it is declared: "You are a priest forever, in the order of Melchizedek."

Once again, Psalm 110 is appealed to in order to demonstrate that the priesthood of the Messiah would be like that of Melchizedek. The point is made that Melchizedek did not become a priest on the basis of his ancestry. He became a priest on the basis of the power of an indestructible life. Whether the lack of genealogy of Melchizedek is taken literally or literarily, it nonetheless points to a Messianic priest to come who would have no beginning of days or end of life.

Jesus demonstrated the power of an indestructible life through the resurrection. His qualification for the priesthood in the order of Melchizedek is the fact that death could not destroy him. He had victory over the grave and demonstrated the power of an indestructible life.

Jesus' Priesthood
Establishes a Better Hope   (7:18-19)

18 The former regulation is set aside because it was weak and useless 19 (for the law made nothing perfect), and a better hope is introduced, by which we draw near to God.

Mankind, throughout the ages, has had a hope of eternal life. Hope can be placed in many religious systems that in reality are hopeless. The religious system that provided the greatest hope throughout the ages was the Levitical system and its law. The author now reiterates the ineffectiveness of that system and calls attention to a better hope.

The Law Set Aside

18 The former regulation is set aside because it was weak and useless 19 (for the law made nothing perfect),

The term former regulation is referring to the law. It is described as weak and useless because it made nothing perfect. The law was never intended to be an end unto itself.

It was to be a tutor to bring one to Christ. Paul makes that point in Galatians 3:

> So the law was put in charge to lead us to Christ that we might be justified by faith. Now that faith has come, we are no longer under the supervision of the law. (Gal 3:24-25)

A New Hope Introduced

and a better hope is introduced, by which we draw near to God.

The law was set aside in favor of faith which provides a much greater hope. Paul identifies that faith in Galatians:

> You are all sons of God through faith in Christ Jesus. (Gal 3:26)

It is faith in Jesus Christ that allows mankind to draw near to God. The Levitical priesthood and the law failed in its ability to remove the obstacle of sin and enable men to draw near to God. Jesus Christ, on the other hand, provides a much better hope. Because of his once-for-all sacrifice, the first-century Hebrews and all mankind can believe in Jesus, have the obstacle of sin removed and draw near to God.

Jesus' Priesthood is Established with God's Oath   (7:20-22)

20 And it was not without an oath! Others became priests without any oath, 21 but he became a priest with an oath when God said to him: "The Lord has sworn and will not change his mind: 'You are a priest forever.'" 22 Because of this oath, Jesus has become the guarantee of a better covenant.

The author continues to add argument upon argument supporting his thesis that the priesthood of the Messiah is superior to the Aaronic priesthood. He returns once again to Psalm 110 to establish the fact that the priesthood of the Messiah was established with an oath.

Priests Appointed without an Oath

20 And it was not without an oath! Others became priests without any oath,

The Aaronic priesthood is established in Exodus, chapter 28, through a command to Moses:

> "Have Aaron your brother brought to you from among the Israelites, with his sons Nadab and Abihu, Eleazar and Ithamar, so that they may serve me as priests. (Ex 28:1)

Moses was told what to do, but there was no oath involved in the establishment of this priesthood.

Jesus Appointed with an Oath

21 but he became a priest with an oath when God said to him: "The Lord has sworn and will not change his mind: 'You are a priest forever.'" 22 Because of this oath, Jesus has become the guarantee of a better covenant.

In establishing the priesthood in the order of Melchizedek, the Lord swore an oath. It guaranteed that God will not change his mind. The plan that he has established is firmly in place and will not change.

The oath also spoke of the Messiah as being a priest forever. Jesus is that Messiah and will be high priest for all eternity.

The author also makes the point that, because of this oath, Jesus is the guarantee of a better covenant. The old covenant consisted of the rules and regulations for approaching God, which were demonstrated to be ineffective because of mankind's sin. The new covenant is also the way in which mankind approaches God, but this is through the shed blood of Jesus. Jesus became the guarantee of that covenant. It is an expression similar to that of a surety bond. In some organizations, employees are insured with a surety bond. This guarantees that if they commit some wrongdoing, the surety company will make good on the loss.

Believers are unable to keep the demands of a holy and righteous God, but Jesus, the believer's surety bond, guarantees that they will not lose the promises because of their sinfulness. He is the guarantee of the better covenant.

Jesus' Priesthood is Established Permanently   (7:23-25)

23 Now there have been many of those priests, since death prevented them from continuing in office; 24 but because Jesus lives forever, he has a permanent priesthood. 25 Therefore he is able to save completely those who come to God through him, because he always lives to intercede for them.

Another aspect of the superiority of the priesthood which Jesus holds is its permanency. He is a priest forever. Through his resurrection he has demonstrated the power of an indestructible life. Death will never end his priesthood.

Aaronic Priests Die

23 Now there have been many of those priests, since death

175

prevented them from continuing in office;

In comparing the Aaronic priesthood to Jesus' priesthood the author reminds his readers that all Aaronic priests die. The death of Aaron, his sons, and many other priests are recorded in Scripture. None of them ever demonstrated the power of an indestructible life.

Jesus Lives Forever

24 but because Jesus lives forever, he has a permanent priesthood. 25 Therefore he is able to save completely those who come to God through him, because he always lives to intercede for them.

Jesus has become a priest on the basis of his indestructible life as demonstrated by the resurrection. This also demonstrates that he will live forever. His eternal life also allows him to serve in a permanent priesthood. It will never end.

Jesus is able to save completely because he is able to intercede at all times. There will never be a time when believers do not have a mediator between God and themselves that is, the Christ, Jesus. He will save all who come to God through him. Jesus made it clear in the upper room that he is the only way to God:

> Jesus answered, "I am the way and the truth and the life. No one comes to the Father except through me. (John 14:6)

Those who come to God through Jesus will be saved completely since Jesus will intercede for them forever.

Jesus' Priesthood
is Established Perfectly   (7:26-28)

26 Such a high priest meets our need—one who is holy, blameless, pure, set apart from sinners, exalted above the heavens. 27 Unlike the other high priests, he does not need to offer sacrifices day after day, first for his own sins, and then for the sins of the people. He sacrificed for their sins once for all when he offered himself. 28 For the law appoints as high priests men who are weak; but the oath, which came after the law, appointed the Son, who has been made perfect forever.

The author ends this chapter with a wonderful description of Jesus the high priest. He is described as being holy, which speaks of personal holiness in all of his actions. He is blameless, meaning there is no evil or malice in him. He is pure which makes him free from that which deforms or defiles. He is set apart and separated unto the Father for the specific purpose of interceding for mankind. He is exalted above the heavens, speaking of his high position and his ability to enter the most holy place of the heavenly tabernacle. This high priest, Jesus, has established the priesthood perfectly.

The Perfect Sacrifice

26 Such a high priest meets our need—one who is holy, blameless, pure, set apart from sinners, exalted above the heavens. 27 Unlike the other high priests, he does not need to offer sacrifices day after day, first for his own sins, and then for the sins of the people. He sacrificed for their sins once for all when he offered himself.

The Aaronic priesthood was characterized by daily activity. Sacrifices were continually made in the temple. It was also characterized by sacrifices for the priests. The priests were sinners and therefore needed to sacrifice for their own sin before they could deal with the sin of the people. Unlike the Aaronic priests, Jesus had no sin and did not need a sacrifice for himself nor did he have to make a sacrifice every day. Instead he presented his own body as the once-for-all sacrifice for all mankind. This sacrifice, brought to the Father, established Jesus as the perfect high priest.

The Perfect Son

> 28 For the law appoints as high priests men who are weak; but the oath, which came after the law, appointed the Son, who has been made perfect forever.

The Aaronic priesthood, established by the law, appointed men who were weak. They were weak both in the fact that they were sinners and also in the fact that they died.

The oath of Psalm 110 that selected the Messiah as a priest appointed a perfect man. Jesus, that man, has demonstrated his power over death and will never die again. He has also demonstrated his moral perfection by experiencing all the temptations of mankind and never sinning.

The priesthood of Jesus is superior because he is the perfect Son of God.

Chapter Twelve

Jesus is a High Priest Entering
a Superior Sanctuary   (8:1 to 8:5)

Jesus' Priesthood is in heaven
in the True Tabernacle   (8:1-3)

1 ¶ The point of what we are saying is this: We do have such a high priest, who sat down at the right hand of the throne of the Majesty in heaven, 2 and who serves in the sanctuary, the true tabernacle set up by the Lord, not by man. 3 Every high priest is appointed to offer both gifts and sacrifices, and so it was necessary for this one also to have something to offer.

The beginning verses of chapter eight are used to summarize the point that has been discussed. In the previous chapter many significant details about the high priestly role of the Messiah were presented. Now the point is made that the high priest and Messiah has come.

The Seated High Priest

1 ¶ The point of what we are saying is this: We do have such a high priest, who sat down at the right hand of the throne of the Majesty in heaven,

The author suggests to his readers that "we" do have such a high priest. He is, of course, speaking of Jesus, who has demonstrated his qualification for priesthood by an indestructible life through the resurrection. The use of the term "we" does not necessarily imply that the Hebrews have put their faith in this high priest. The point is that the high priest is there and the Hebrews are invited to go to him in faith.

A few significant details concerning this priest are given. First of all, he sat down. High priests always stood to do their work. There were never any chairs in the sanctuary. The fact that this high priest sat down demonstrates that his work was completed. Unlike the Aaronic priests, he does not have to prepare sacrifices day after day.

He sat at the right hand. This location is the position of authority. It demonstrates that this high priest has been given the most important position in the universe.

He is seated by the Majesty in heaven. This demonstrates his intimacy with the God of the universe. Priests in the earth realm never had a sense of closeness to God. They went into his presence once a year with great fear and trembling. This high priest, instead was at peace with God and able to make intercession for mankind.

The True Tabernacle

2 and who serves in the sanctuary, the true tabernacle set up by the Lord, not by man. 3 Every high priest is appointed to offer both gifts and sacrifices, and so it was necessary for this one also to have something to offer.

Although God is omnipresent, the tabernacle has been the place where he manifests his presence for mankind. The true tabernacle, however, is in heaven. This is the place where Jesus serves in order for it to be possible for mankind to be in the presence of God in heaven.

This true tabernacle was set up by God, not by man. The tabernacle in the wilderness was built by Moses. It was followed by temples built by Solomon, Zerubbabel, and Herod. The heavenly tabernacle is different. It was totally established by the Lord.

The high priest who served in the earthly tabernacle brought gifts and sacrifices. Likewise, the high priest who serves in the heavenly tabernacle had to have something to offer. Jesus, the high priest, offered his own body, a sinless sacrifice; the perfect lamb of God. No other sacrifice would ever be needed; the sacrifice of Jesus was the once-for-all sacrifice for sin.

Jesus' Priesthood is not on Earth in the Shadow of the Tabernacle (8:4-5)

4 If he were on earth, he would not be a priest, for there are already men who offer the gifts prescribed by the law. 5 They serve at a sanctuary that is a copy and shadow of what is in heaven. This is why Moses was warned when he was about to build the tabernacle: "See to it that you make everything according to the pattern shown you on the mountain."

The service of Jesus in the true tabernacle of heaven is contrasted with the service of men in the copy of the tabernacle on earth. Copies of paintings by great artists like Rembrandt can be found everywhere. They are reproduced in books, pamphlets and hang on people's walls. The copies are relatively worthless compared to the original. An original painting by Rembrandt would be a great treasure.

In the same way, copies of the tabernacle do not have the value of the true tabernacle in heaven. The tabernacle at which the Messiah, Jesus, serves is superior to any on earth.

The Shadow

4 If he were on earth, he would not be a priest, for there are already men who offer the gifts prescribed by the law. 5 They serve at a sanctuary that is a copy and shadow of what is in heaven.

Inasmuch as Jesus came from the tribe of Judah, not Levi, he was not qualified to be a priest on the earth. The appointment of earthly priests was on the basis of God's command in the law. Only a descendant of Aaron could serve as the priest. Jesus did not qualify.

The priests made their offerings in accordance with the law, which was previously shown to be a tutor to bring one to Christ. The law was ineffective to deal with man's sin problem and bring him near to God. The Messianic high priest, on the other hand, was able to do that.

The sanctuary in which earthly high priests served was described as a copy and shadow of what is in heaven. A shadow may look very much like the object which is casting the shadow, but it is far inferior. A shadow has no enduring existence of its own. If a cloud passes in front of the sun, the shadow disappears. The sanctuary in heaven is that which is lasting and of great value.

The Reality

5b This is why Moses was warned when he was about to build the tabernacle: "See to it that you make everything according to the pattern shown you on the mountain."

Exodus chapter 25 reveals that Moses was given a pattern for the tabernacle:

> See that you make them according to the pattern shown you on the mountain. (Ex 25:40)

Hebrews adds the information that this pattern represented a copy of what was in heaven. Inasmuch as Moses was dealing with duplicating a heavenly tabernacle, his work had to be precise. To ensure that the work was done properly, the Lord filled some of the tabernacle workers with his Spirit:

> Then the LORD said to Moses, "See I have chosen Bezalel son of Uri, the son of Hur, of the tribe of Judah, and I have filled him with the Spirit of God, with skill, ability and knowledge in all kinds of crafts—to make artistic designs for work in gold, silver and bronze, to cut and set stones, to work in wood, and to engage in all kinds of craftsmanship. Moreover, I have appointed Oholiab son of Ahisamach, of the tribe of Dan, to help him. Also I have given skill to all the craftsmen to make everything I have commanded you. (Ex 31:1-6)

In this manner, the Holy Spirit superintended the building of the tabernacle just as today he superintends the building of the church.

The arguments that Jesus is a superior high priest are compelling. This superior high priest serving in a superior sanctuary is the administrator of a superior covenant. The author of Hebrews next draws attention to the covenant Jesus administers.

Chapter Thirteen

Jesus is a High Priest Administering a Superior Covenant   (8:6 To 9:15)

The Need for A Better Covenant   (8:6-9)

6 ¶ But the ministry Jesus has received is as superior to theirs as the covenant of which he is mediator is superior to the old one, and it is founded on better promises. 7 For if there had been nothing wrong with that first covenant, no place would have been sought for another. 8 But God found fault with the people and said: "The time is coming, declares the Lord, when I will make a new covenant with the house of Israel and with the house of Judah. 9 It will not be like the covenant I made with their forefathers when I took them by the hand to lead them out of Egypt, because they did not remain faithful to my covenant, and I turned away from them, declares the Lord.

The recipients of this letter were Hebrews saved under the old covenant by faith in the coming Messiah. The author has demonstrated the superiority of Jesus to the angels, the prophets, and the priests. He now discusses the superiority of the covenant of which Jesus is the mediator.

The goal of any mediator is to bring two parties together. The priestly system had as its objectives to bring men close to God and to take away their sin. Neither of these objectives were met in the old covenant system. The Hebrews remained outside the temple while the high priest went in to draw close to God. The Hebrews' sin was never taken away by the blood of animals. Both of these problems are dealt with in the author's discussion of the new covenant.

The Old Covenant Needed to be Replaced

6 ¶ But the ministry Jesus has received is as superior to theirs as the covenant of which he is mediator is superior to the old one, and it is founded on better promises. 7 For if there had been nothing wrong with that first covenant, no place would have been sought for another. 8 But God found fault with the people...

The discussion begins by stating that the new covenant is founded on better promises then the old. In essence, the promises are to achieve the two goals of a priestly system. The first goal is to bring men close to God. The new covenant promises, "I will be their God and they will be my people" (Heb 8:10). The people, from the greatest to the least, will draw near to God.

The second promise is, "For I will forgive their wickedness and will remember their sins no more." (Heb 8:12) The problem of people's sin was dealt with once and for all by the new covenant in Christ's blood.

The author makes the point that the first covenant had to be deficient or there would not have been a need for a second covenant. The wording is similar to Hebrews 7:11:

> If perfection could have been attained through the Levitical priesthood (for on the basis of it the law was given to the people), why was there still need for another priest to come—one in the order of Melchizedek, not in the order of Aaron? (Heb 7:11)

The point in chapter 7 was that the Levitical priesthood

was ineffective and needed to be replaced by a better priesthood. The point being made in chapter 8 is that the covenant was ineffective and needed to be replaced by a new covenant.

The ineffectiveness of the covenant was not due to its nature, rather the inability of people to comply with it. From the very onset God had reason to find fault with the people. The account of the law being given in Exodus 32 includes a description of God's anger:

> Then the LORD said to Moses, "Go down, because your people, whom you brought up out of Egypt, have become corrupt. They have been quick to turn away from what I commanded them and have made themselves an idol cast in the shape of a calf. They have bowed down to it and sacrificed to it and have said, 'These are your gods, O Israel, who brought you up out of Egypt.' "I have seen these people," the LORD said to Moses, "and they are a stiff-necked people. Now leave me alone so that my anger may burn against them and that I may destroy them. Then I will make you into a great nation." (Ex 32:7-10)

It was obvious on the first day the law was given that the people were not going to have the ability to follow it. The law, that is, the old covenant, was therefore not going to be effective and would need to be replaced by another covenant.

The New Covenant had been Promised

... and said: "The time is coming, declares the Lord, when I will make a new covenant with the house of Israel and with the house of Judah. 9 It will not be like the covenant I made with

their forefathers when I took them by the hand to lead them out of Egypt, because they did not remain faithful to my covenant, and I turned away from them, declares the Lord.

The new covenant was not something that God thought of in the first century. It was always his intention to provide an unconditional covenant that he would be responsible for fulfilling. The author of Hebrews quotes from Jeremiah 31 in order to make the point that the covenant had been promised to the forefathers of the Hebrews.

Previously, the author had demonstrated that a new priesthood had been prophesied. He did this by quoting Psalm 110. Now he is demonstrating that with the change of the priesthood there is also a change of the law. He shows that a new law, that is a new covenant, had also been prophesied.

In describing the giving of the old covenant, the author speaks of taking Israel by the hand to lead them out of Egypt. The picture is that of a child being led. This is the same picture that Paul uses in describing the purpose of the old covenant to the church at Galatia. He says it is a tutor to lead people to Christ. Tutors typically worked with young children who needed to be led by the hand.

The problem with the old covenant is that people did not remain faithful to it; therefore, God turned away from them. Once again one sees an expression of the two goals of the priesthood: to deal with sin and to bring people near to God. Not being faithful to the covenant meant people were sinning. God turning away from them makes it impossible for men to get close to God. The old covenant was ineffective.

The Description of
The Better Covenant (8:10-13)

10 This is the covenant I will make with the house of Israel after that time, declares the Lord. I will put my laws in their minds and write them on their hearts. I will be their God, and they will be my people. 11 No longer will a man teach his neighbor, or a man his brother, saying, 'Know the Lord,' because they will all know me, from the least of them to the greatest. 12 For I will forgive their wickedness and will remember their sins no more." 13 By calling this covenant "new," he has made the first one obsolete; and what is obsolete and aging will soon disappear.

The author continues to quote from Jeremiah 31 as he describes the new covenant. The covenant began at the death and resurrection of Jesus. Israel will experience the fulfillment of the covenant during the millennial reign of Christ. Meanwhile, between the first coming of Jesus and his return, the church is formed.

The Nature of the New Covenant

10 This is the covenant I will make with the house of Israel after that time, declares the Lord. I will put my laws in their minds and write them on their hearts. I will be their God, and they will be my people.

The new covenant was made with Israel. Some mistakenly believe that the old covenant was for Israel and the new covenant was for the church. Jeremiah and the author of Hebrews make it clear that the new covenant was made with the house of Israel.

Gentiles can participate in the new covenant as engrafted olive branches. Paul uses this metaphor in Romans chapter 11. Israel is described as a cultivated olive tree and the Gentiles are described as wild olive branches. The wild branches are engrafted into the cultivated tree. Paul prophecies a day when cultivated olive branches will again be engrafted into the cultivated tree. This describes

Israel's turning to Christ at the time of his second coming.

The nature of the new covenant is described in two ways. First, I will put my laws on their minds and, second, I will be their God. Clearly this deals with the two goals of a priestly system. First, to deal with people's sin and second, to bring people close to God.

Obviously, laws written on the heart have the ability to convict of sin in a way that an external code, that is, the law, cannot. The law being written on the hearts implies the indwelling of the Holy Spirit. He is able to convict the world of guilt in regard to sin and righteousness and judgment. (John 16:8)

"I will be their God and they will be my people" points to the millennial kingdom. The Messianic king, Jesus, will reign at Jerusalem and will be Emmanuel, meaning "God with us."

The Results of the New Covenant

11 No longer will a man teach his neighbor, or a man his brother, saying, 'Know the Lord,' because they will all know me, from the least of them to the greatest. 12 For I will forgive their wickedness and will remember their sins no more."

The results of the new covenant are as one would expect. Mankind is able to draw close to God and the sin problem is taken care of. The concept of everyone knowing God describes conditions in the millennial kingdom. Inasmuch as Jesus will be a worldwide king reigning in Jerusalem, the entire world will know him. All mankind will have the information they need in order to be drawn close to God.

The forgiveness of wickedness and forgetting of sin was accomplished at the cross. This is when the new covenant was put into effect.

The Obsolescence of the Old Covenant

13 By calling this covenant "new," he has made the first one obsolete; and what is obsolete and aging will soon disappear.

This is one of the most interesting verses in the book of Hebrews. It calls the old covenant obsolete and aging. Something that is obsolete and aging can still work. Computers are obsolete as soon as the newer models come out. Nonetheless, people operate with obsolete computers for years before they upgrade to the newer technology.

This wording would imply that in some way the old covenant was still operational at the time of the writing of the Hebrews. This is consistent with the next phrase that says the old covenant "will soon disappear." The Hebrew readers would have to wonder what was going to transpire that would cause the old covenant to disappear. It was likely that they could see the growing opposition from Rome and understood that their temple and sacrificial system was in jeopardy.

In the year 70 AD, the Romans destroyed the temple at Jerusalem, burning it to the ground, and leaving no stone unturned. At that point the old covenant, with its temple worship and sacrificial system, disappeared.

The new covenant went into effect at the point of Jesus' death and resurrection which was approximately 30 AD. The old covenant disappeared at the destruction of the temple in 70 AD. During the forty years between those two dates, the old covenant is described as obsolete and aging.

This obsolete and aging system was still operative for some period. Perhaps there were people saved under the old covenant by faith in the coming Messiah who died before they found out the Messiah had come. In that scenario, their old covenant salvation was sufficient.

Many Hebrews saved under the old covenant were exposed to the teaching about Jesus. Once they had been enlightened, if they turned away, they could not be brought back to repentance. (Heb 6:4-6) They were declaring that they agreed with the decision to crucify Jesus as a false Messiah. The writer of Hebrews says, "They are crucifying the Son of God all over again and subjecting him to public disgrace."

To state it clearly, I believe that the Hebrews' old covenant salvation could be lost once they were enlightened as to who Jesus was and turned away from him. This understanding eliminates one of the great debates of the book of Hebrews as to whether someone can lose his salvation or not.

New Testament believers are not able to lose their salvation because they are indwelt with the Holy Spirit, as a guarantee of their inheritance. (Eph 1:13-14) No such indwelling or guarantee was given to Old Testament saints. During the unique forty-year period from 30 AD to 70 AD it was possible for a saved Old Testament saint to lose his salvation because he rejected the Messiah who had come, that is, Jesus.

The whole purpose of the book of Hebrews was to persuade the Hebrews to believe in Jesus and not turn away from him. If they did turn away, they couldn't go back to the old sacrificial system.

In 70 AD when the temple was destroyed, the forty-year window of opportunity closed. No longer could anyone be saved by faith in a coming Messiah. They could only be saved by faith in Jesus, the Messiah who has come. Those Hebrews who do not put their faith in Jesus are like the Israelites who died in the wilderness following the Exodus. During those forty years, the very people who were lead out of Egypt, never made it to the promised land because of their unbelief.

The Description of
the Earthly Sanctuary   (9:1-5)

1 ¶ Now the first covenant had regulations for worship and also an earthly sanctuary. 2 A tabernacle was set up. In its first room were the lampstand, the table and the consecrated bread; this was called the Holy Place. 3 Behind the second curtain was a room called the Most Holy Place, 4 which had the golden altar of incense and the gold-covered ark of the covenant. This ark contained the gold jar of manna, Aaron's staff that had budded, and the stone tablets of the covenant. 5 Above the ark were the cherubim of the Glory, overshadowing the atonement cover. But we cannot discuss these things in detail now.

The high priest ministering under the old covenant did his work in an earthly sanctuary while Jesus the high priest does his work in a heavenly sanctuary. In demonstrating the superiority of Jesus, the author does not rip apart the earthly sanctuary and its function, instead he builds it up. In so doing, he demonstrates that since the earthly sanctuary was a glorious place, the sanctuary in heaven must be all the more glorious.

The Holy Place

1 ¶ Now the first covenant had regulations for worship and also an earthly sanctuary. 2 A tabernacle was set up. In its first room were the lampstand, the table and the consecrated bread; this was called the Holy Place.

The temple is described in detail in Exodus, chapters 25 through 40. In Hebrews, there is but a brief overview of its two most important locations. It begins with the Holy Place which was only entered by priests. Two pieces of furniture are identified in the Holy Place. The first is the golden lampstand. It had seven branches and was filled with the purest olive oil. Its ability to give light is metaphorically a picture of Jesus Christ who said he was the light of the world.

The second piece of furniture is the table of consecrated bread. Jesus also proclaimed that he was the bread of life.

The Most Holy Place

3 Behind the second curtain was a room called the Most Holy Place, 4 which had the golden altar of incense and the gold-covered ark of the covenant. This ark contained the gold jar of manna, Aaron's staff that had budded, and the stone tablets of the covenant. 5 Above the ark were the cherubim of the Glory, overshadowing the atonement cover. But we cannot discuss these things in detail now.

Beyond the Holy Place was a section called the Most Holy Place. It was the location where God chose to manifest his presence. The Most Holy Place was separated from the Holy Place by a curtain. Only the high priest could enter the Most Holy Place and he could do that only once a year—on the Day of Atonement.

At the death of Jesus, the veil (curtain) of the temple was torn from top to bottom. This signified that the way to God was open. The curtain that separated mankind from the Most Holy Place was now torn and allowed mankind to draw near to God. This will be dealt with further in the book of Hebrews.

In the Most Holy Place was the golden altar of incense. This was a picture of Jesus interceding on behalf of mankind. The altar was right in front of the gold-covered ark of the covenant.

The ark was a box with a cover on it. Inside the ark were three articles of importance in Israel's history. The first was a golden jar of manna to remember how the Lord fed them in the wilderness. The second was Aaron's rod that had budded in order to demonstrate that he was the high priest appointed by God. The third item was the stone tablets of the covenant, which were the 10 commandments given to Moses on the mountain.

The ark had two cherubim overshadowing the cover. The cherubim were angelic figures made of gold. This was the place where God met with man as described in Exodus 25:

> There, above the cover between the two cherubim that are over the ark of the Testimony, I will meet with you and give you all my commands for the Israelites. (Ex 25:22)

The atonement cover, or mercy seat, as translated in the King James Version, was the place where the blood of the atonement day sacrifice was brought.

In 1 John, chapter two, Jesus is said to be mankind's propitiation:

> And he is the propitiation for our sins: and not for ours only, but also for [the sins of] the whole world. (1 John 2:2)

The Greek word translated "propitiation" is rendered "mercy seat" in the Septuagint translation of Exodus 25:17. In utilizing the same Greek word for Jesus role and for the mercy seat, the Septuagint translators have concluded rightly that Jesus is mankind's mercy seat.

The Description of
Priestly Activity   (9:6-7)

6 When everything had been arranged like this, the priests entered regularly into the outer room to carry on their ministry.
7 But only the high priest entered the inner room, and that

only once a year, and never without blood, which he offered for himself and for the sins the people had committed in ignorance.

Having described the two rooms within the sanctuary, the author now describes the two classes of priests.

Priests Enter Holy Place

6 When everything had been arranged like this, the priests entered regularly into the outer room to carry on their ministry.

The priests went into the Holy Place daily in order to perform their ministry. They would trim the lights on the lampstand and change the consecrated bread on the table. There were no seats in the sanctuary as an indication that the priest's work was never completed.

High Priest Enters Most Holy Place

7 But only the high priest entered the inner room, and that only once a year, and never without blood, which he offered for himself and for the sins the people had committed in ignorance.

Once a year, on the Day of Atonement (Yom Kippur), the high priest entered into the Most Holy Place. He entered with blood, first for himself and then for the sins of the people. The entire ritual of the Day of Atonement is described in Leviticus, chapter 16.

The sacrifice made for the people on that day involved two goats. The first goat was killed and his blood brought into the Most Holy Place and sprinkled on the mercy seat.

The high priest laid his hands on the second goat and confessed the sins of the people. The second goat was then sent out into the wilderness never to return. He was symbolically removing sin from the nation of Israel.

In this one sacrifice, involving two goats, the two goals of the priesthood were to be achieved. The first goat was thought to allow priests to bring mankind close to God. The second goat was thought to allow the priest to deal with mankind's sin problem.

These activities were just pictures of the Messiah to come. When Jesus died, he supplied his own blood to bring mankind into the Most Holy Place and dealt with the sin problem once and for all when he became sin for us.

The Ineffectiveness of Animal Sacrifices (9:8-10)

8 ¶ The Holy Spirit was showing by this that the way into the Most Holy Place had not yet been disclosed as long as the first tabernacle was still standing. 9 This is an illustration for the present time, indicating that the gifts and sacrifices being offered were not able to clear the conscience of the worshipper. 10 They are only a matter of food and drink and various ceremonial washings—external regulations applying until the time of the new order.

After describing the sanctuary and the priests, the author draws attention to the gifts and sacrifices themselves. They are demonstrated to be only temporary and ineffective.

Way to the Most Holy Place not Disclosed

8 ¶ The Holy Spirit was showing by this that the way into the Most Holy Place had not yet been disclosed as long as the first tabernacle was still standing.

No one could enter the Most Holy Place without a blood sacrifice. But even with a blood sacrifice the way to the Most Holy Place was very limited. It was limited to only

197

one man, the high priest, and it was limited to only one day a year, Yom Kippur. This very limited access to God hardly achieves the goal of the priesthood which is to bring men close to God. The real way to God had not yet been disclosed until Jesus died and rose. His sacrifice and the blood of the new covenant would provide unlimited access to those who believe.

The temple and its sacrifices not only were limited in providing access but also were temporary. In speaking of the tabernacle still standing, the author is implying that it will not always stand. He has previously stated that the old covenant is obsolete and aging and will soon disappear. Along with the old covenant will go the tabernacle. Its destruction will come a few years after the book of Hebrews was written.

Sacrifices were an Illustration

9 This is an illustration for the present time, indicating that the gifts and sacrifices being offered were not able to clear the conscience of the worshipper. 10 They are only a matter of food and drink and various ceremonial washings—external regulations applying until the time of the new order.

The primary purpose of sacrifices was to be a picture of the ultimate sacrifice to be made by Jesus. In addition to pointing to that, they also, by their nature, pointed to their own ineffectiveness. They were ineffective in that they were not able to clear the conscience of the worshipper. The conscience is an internal problem and therefore needs an internal solution. That solution would come as part of the new covenant. The new covenant writes the law on the heart. The indwelling Holy Spirit is able to clear the conscience of the new covenant worshipper.

Under the old covenant, regulations were merely external. Just as the law was external, so also the ceremonial acts performed were all external. These external activities were only temporary until the time of the new order. The time of the new order refers to the new covenant.

Once the new covenant was in place these external regulations, dealing with food, drink, and ceremonial washings, were to be eliminated. Their value as an illustration was complete once that which they were illustrating came to pass. When the once-for-all sacrifice of Jesus was made, the illustration was unnecessary.

The Reality of the Messiah's Sacrifice (9:11-12)

11 When Christ came as high priest of the good things that are already here, he went through the greater and more perfect tabernacle that is not man-made, that is to say, not a part of this creation. 12 He did not enter by means of the blood of goats and calves; but he entered the Most Holy Place once for all by his own blood, having obtained eternal redemption.

Having discussed the ineffectiveness of animal sacrifices the author now contrasts the effectiveness of the Messiah's sacrifice. The New International Version uses the expression "when Christ came;" however, it is literally "but Christ came." The word "but" provides a strong contrast between the ineffectiveness of animal sacrifices and the total effectiveness of Jesus' sacrifice.

The Greater Tabernacle

11 When Christ came as high priest of the good things that are already here, he went through the greater and more perfect tabernacle that is not man-made, that is to say, not a part of this creation.

Once again, the reader is reminded that the Messiah (Christ) is a high priest. Since Jesus is the Messiah who has come, the good things were already here. The illustrations, the shadows, the types, were no longer necessary. The fulfillment of all of these was already here.

Even the tabernacle as a type is unnecessary. Jesus, the Messiah, has gone through a greater and more perfect tabernacle. He has entered into the heavenly places. The tabernacle that he entered was not temporal, but eternal. It was not manmade; not part of this creation. It was rather in the very presence of God and eternal.

The Greater Sacrifice

12 He did not enter by means of the blood of goats and calves; but he entered the Most Holy Place once for all by his own blood, having obtained eternal redemption.

The blood of goats and calves had previously been demonstrated to be ineffective. Jesus did not enter with such blood. Instead he brought his own blood. His blood was sinless and divine. Through the miracle of the virgin birth, Jesus had no sin nature passed along to him from Adam. Likewise, he did not sin during his time on the earth.

Jesus blood, not tainted by sin, was the perfect sacrifice. The fact that Jesus was Divine allowed that sacrifice to be sufficient, not just for one man, but for all mankind. His sacrifice was once for all. No other sacrifice could add to what Jesus has already accomplished at Calvary.

The Effectiveness of the Messiah's Sacrifice (9:13-15)

13 The blood of goats and bulls and the ashes of a heifer sprinkled on those who are ceremonially unclean sanctify them so that they are outwardly clean. 14 How much more, then, will the blood of Christ, who through the eternal Spirit offered himself unblemished to God, cleanse our consciences from acts that lead to death, so that we may serve the living God! 15 ¶ For this reason Christ is the mediator of a new covenant, that those who are called may receive the promised eternal inheritance—now that he has died as a ransom to set them free from the sins committed under the first covenant.

The author goes on to solidify the point that Jesus' sacrifice is totally effective. Once again, he draws the comparison of the blood of animals and the blood of Christ. He does this using an argument from the lesser to the greater.

The Blood of Goats

13 The blood of goats and bulls and the ashes of a heifer sprinkled on those who are ceremonially unclean sanctify them so that they are outwardly clean.

In making his argument, the author concludes that there is value in the blood of goats and bulls. They were an effective outward ceremony in order to make someone outwardly clean. While their value was limited in scope, it was able to accomplish what it was designed for.

The Blood of Christ

14 How much more, then, will the blood of Christ, who through the eternal Spirit offered himself unblemished to God, cleanse our consciences from acts that lead to death, so that we may serve the living God! 15 ¶ For this reason Christ is the mediator of a new covenant, that those who are called may receive the promised eternal inheritance—now that he has died as a ransom to set them free from the sins committed under the first covenant.

If animal blood could have the effectiveness to make someone clean externally, how much more would the blood of the Messiah be effective in what it was designed for, that is, to deal internally with the consciences of men. The blood of Christ was unblemished. It was not tainted by sin. Christ's blood was offered by himself. He was not simply put on the cross because the Jews and Romans desired it. He was put on the cross because he was the lamb slain before the foundations of the world. In eternity past it was planned that Jesus would sacrifice himself.

Notice that his sacrifice accomplished two things. First, it cleansed the conscience, which is another way of saying it dealt with the sin problem. The second thing it did was allow people to serve the living God; in other words, they could draw close to God. These are the goals of the priesthood.

With the Messiah being the mediator of the new covenant, the author makes the point that he has achieved the two goals of the priesthood. The writer says, "Those who are called may receive the promised eternal inheritance." They may draw close to God. He also says, "he (Christ) has died as a ransom to set them free from the sins committed under the first covenant." He has dealt with the sin problem.

The blood of Christ has been totally effective in meeting the goals of the high priestly system.

Chapter Fourteen

Jesus is a High Priest Shedding
Superior Blood   (9:16 to 9:28)

The Blood of the Old Covenant
Covered Sin   (9:16-22)

16 In the case of a will, it is necessary to prove the death of the one who made it, 17 because a will is in force only when somebody has died; it never takes effect while the one who made it is living. 18 This is why even the first covenant was not put into effect without blood. 19 When Moses had proclaimed every commandment of the law to all the people, he took the blood of calves, together with water, scarlet wool and branches of hyssop, and sprinkled the scroll and all the people. 20 He said, "This is the blood of the covenant, which God has commanded you to keep." 21 In the same way, he sprinkled with the blood both the tabernacle and everything used in its ceremonies. 22 In fact, the law requires that nearly everything be cleansed with blood, and without the shedding of blood there is no forgiveness.

The importance of blood in the sacrificial system is further emphasized by the continuing discussion of the subject. The focus begins with the old covenant and its use of blood to cover sin and then moves to the new covenant and its use of blood to remove sin.

A Will Requires Death to become Effective

16 In the case of a will, it is necessary to prove the death of the

*one who made it, 17 because a will is in force only when some-
body has died; it never takes effect while the one who made it is
living.*

All the promises of the new covenant are for heirs;
therefore, the mediator of the covenant had to die before
believers could inherit the promises. The inheritance
revealed in the will could not be distributed until the
Messiah died.

Many times a will adds a stipulation to the inheritance.
Sometimes it will say that a person has to reach a certain
age, or be married, or enter a certain profession, before they
can inherit the estate. There is a stipulation in the new
covenant, as well. It is that one believe on the Lord Jesus
Christ.

Blood was Sprinkled on Everything

*18 This is why even the first covenant was not put into effect
without blood. 19 When Moses had proclaimed every
commandment of the law to all the people, he took the blood of
calves, together with water, scarlet wool and branches of
hyssop, and sprinkled the scroll and all the people. 20 He said,
"This is the blood of the covenant, which God has commanded
you to keep." 21 In the same way, he sprinkled with the blood
both the tabernacle and everything used in its ceremonies.*

The old covenant did not convey the inheritance to the
heirs. Only Jesus' blood, given as part of the new covenant,
could accomplish that. Nonetheless, the old covenant was to
be a type and a picture of what was to come. Therefore,
even the first covenant required blood. The blood of animals
was to be a reminder that a sacrifice was necessary in order
to deal with man's sin. From the day Israel received the law
at Mount Sinai, blood was used in their worship. Moses

sprinkled blood on the scroll, the people, the tabernacle and everything used in its ceremonies.

Shed Blood Required for Forgiveness

22 In fact, the law requires that nearly everything be cleansed with blood, and without the shedding of blood there is no forgiveness.

All of the use of blood by Moses and those who would follow him through the years, was to demonstrate that, without the shedding of blood, there was no forgiveness. Anyone who thinks that Jesus could have saved the world without dying is greatly mistaken. His blood was necessary for the redemption of mankind. The entire old covenant with its bloody sacrifices pointed to this once-for-all sacrifice of the Messiah for the sins of man.

The Blood of the New Covenant
Removed Sin   (9:23-28)

23 ¶ It was necessary, then, for the copies of the heavenly things to be purified with these sacrifices, but the heavenly things themselves with better sacrifices than these. 24 For Christ did not enter a man-made sanctuary that was only a copy of the true one; he entered heaven itself, now to appear for us in God's presence. 25 Nor did he enter heaven to offer himself again and again, the way the high priest enters the Most Holy Place every year with blood that is not his own. 26 Then Christ would have had to suffer many times since the creation of the world. But now he has appeared once for all at the end of the ages to do away with sin by the sacrifice of himself. 27 Just as man is destined to die once, and after that to face judgment, 28 so Christ was sacrificed once to take away the sins of many people; and he will appear a second time, not to bear sin, but to bring salvation to those who are waiting for him.

Throughout its years of operation and its innumerable sacrifices, the old covenant covered sin but was not able to remove it. The new covenant, on the other hand, removed sin. It removed it through the sacrifice of the perfect mediator, Jesus.

Christ Entered Heaven with his Blood

23 ¶ It was necessary, then, for the copies of the heavenly things to be purified with these sacrifices, but the heavenly things themselves with better sacrifices than these. 24 For Christ did not enter a man-made sanctuary that was only a copy of the true one; he entered heaven itself, now to appear for us in God's presence.

On the Day of Atonement, the high priest would use the blood of the sacrifice for cleansing utensils in the temple and for sprinkling on the Mercy Seat in the Most Holy Place.

If it was necessary for the earthly high priest to utilize blood in this process, how much more for our heavenly high priest. The important distinction here is the effectiveness of the blood, not the things to be purified. There are many questions as to what needs purification in heaven. Hughes captures the import of this activity:

> "There is no need to seek precise and detailed parallels and correspondences between the cleansing ritual with its multiplicity of applications under the old system and the purification which is made available under the new period. The former is complex

and repetitious, the later simple and compre-
hensive in its uniqueness. Our author's main
intention is to emphasize the absolute superiority of the blood of the new covenant over
that of the old." (Hughes p 381)

On the Day of Atonement, the high priest made three
appearances. He appeared at the brazen altar to perform the
necessary sacrifice. Then he appeared before God in the
Most Holy Place to present the blood of the sacrifice. Lastly
he appeared before the people and they rejoiced that atonement for their sin had been made.

The first use of the word "appear" in verse 24 described
Jesus as the high priest appearing before God. This appearance is presented first by the author of Hebrews even though
it chronologically follows Jesus sacrifice which is presented
next. Just as the earthly high priest brought the blood of the
sacrifice into the Most Holy Place, so also Jesus brought his
own blood into the very presence of God. Jesus did not have
to enter heaven once a year to bring a sacrifice the way the
earthly high priest did. His sacrifice was brought in to the
Father only this one time.

Christ was Sacrificed Only Once

*25 Nor did he enter heaven to offer himself again and again,
the way the high priest enters the Most Holy Place every year
with blood that is not his own. 26 Then Christ would have had
to suffer many times since the creation of the world. But now
he has appeared once for all at the end of the ages to do away
with sin by the sacrifice of himself. 27 Just as man is destined
to die once, and after that to face judgment, 28 so Christ was
sacrificed once to take away the sins of many people;*

The second use of the word "appear" in verse 26

described the appearance of Jesus as the sacrifice. This was the equivalent of the high priest appearing at the brazen altar. The place of sacrifice for Jesus was not the brazen altar but the cross of Calvary. The author makes the point that man is destined to die once and face judgment; therefore, Christ had to die only once to deal with the issue of judgment.

Christ will Return to Bring Salvation

28b and he will appear a second time, not to bear sin, but to bring salvation to those who are waiting for him.

The third use of the word "appear" in this section refers to Jesus' second coming. He appeared before mankind the first time as a sacrifice at Calvary. He then appeared before God with his blood. He will appear before man a second time. The second time he appears is not as a sacrifice but rather to bring the culmination of salvation to those who are waiting for him. Those who are believers in Jesus, the Messiah who has come, will have their salvation complete when he appears.

Chapter Fifteen

Jesus is a High Priest Offering a Superior Sacrifice   (10:1 to 10:18)

The Need for the Lamb of God   (10:1-4)

1 ¶ The law is only a shadow of the good things that are coming— not the realities themselves. For this reason it can never, by the same sacrifices repeated endlessly year after year, make perfect those who draw near to worship. 2 If it could, would they not have stopped being offered? For the worshippers would have been cleansed once for all, and would no longer have felt guilty for their sins. 3 But those sacrifices are an annual reminder of sins, 4 because it is impossible for the blood of bulls and goats to take away sins.

The purpose of any priesthood, with its laws and animal sacrifices, is to allow a worshiper to accomplish two things previously mentioned. First, it is to allow the worshiper to draw near to his God. Second, it is to eliminate the problem of sin.

The author of Hebrews begins chapter ten by demonstrating that the law and its animal sacrifices did not accomplish either of these important goals.

Under the old covenant of the law, the Israelites drew near to worship God. They were not, however, allowed to enter the Holy Place where only priests went, or the Most Holy Place where only the high priest went. In effect, the system kept them away from the presence of God. The law could never make them perfect; therefore, they could never enter God's presence.

The Law could not Bring one Near to God

1 ¶ The law is only a shadow of the good things that are coming— not the realities themselves. For this reason it can never, by the same sacrifices repeated endlessly year after year, make perfect those who draw near to worship. 2 If it could, would they not have stopped being offered? For the worshippers would have been cleansed once for all, and would no longer have felt guilty for their sins.

The Lord did have a system in mind where people could come into his presence but the law was not it. The law was a shadow of the good things that were coming.

A shadow bears a resemblance to the reality, but it falls far short of what the reality is. The reality is Jesus, the perfect man, the eternal high priest, the suitable sacrifice that would bring men to God.

The author argues that, if the sacrifices under the law had been effective, they would have stopped. If worshipers were ever cleansed once for all, their sin problem would be dealt with and they would be able to enter into God's presence.

Animal Sacrifices could not Take Away Sin

3 But those sacrifices are an annual reminder of sins, 4 because it is impossible for the blood of bulls and goats to take away sins.

The sacrificial system did not take away sin. It had the opposite effect, that is, it reminded people of their sin. The annual Day of Atonement ceremony reminded each individual of his own sinfulness. The effect of the high priest's activity on that day was to cover the sin but never deal with the problem.

The reason the problem could not be dealt with is that the blood of bulls and goats could not take away sin. These sacrifices were never able to deal with the sin problem. Only the sacrifice of a perfect man could deal with the problem of sin.

The Obedience of the Lamb of God   (10:5-7)

5 Therefore, when Christ came into the world, he said: "Sacrifice and offering you did not desire, but a body you prepared for me; 6 with burnt offerings and sin offerings you were not pleased. 7 ¶ Then I said, 'Here I am—it is written about me in the scroll—I have come to do your will, O God.'"

The author moves from the ineffectiveness of animal sacrifices to God's provision of the perfect sacrifice. The perfect sacrifice was the Messiah. When the text uses the term Christ, remember, that it is using a Greek term meaning the Messiah. Before even mentioning the name Jesus, the author is going to show that the Messiah was always intended to be the one who would take away sin.

Christ Presented His own Body

5 Therefore, when Christ came into the world, he said: "Sacrifice and offering you did not desire, but a body you prepared for me; 6 with burnt offerings and sin offerings you were not pleased.

The author had previously argued that the new covenant has replaced the old covenant. At this point, he focuses on the most important portion of that covenant, the Messiah's body. He quotes from the 40th Psalm which reads as if the

Messiah were talking to his Father, God. By using this Old Testament text, the author is able to demonstrate to his readers that God was not pleased with nor did he desire sacrifice and offering. God did command that sacrifices and offerings be made, and he was pleased with worshipers who desired to do his will, but the sacrifices in and of themselves were meaningless. The Lord did not depend on the sacrifices of man for anything he needed. Sacrifices could never bring men close to God.

The Messiah, on the other hand, could bring men close to God. In order for that to happen, the Messiah would have to have a man's body that could be sacrificed on behalf of mankind. Psalm 40, written a thousand years before Christ, demonstrated to the Hebrews that this was always God's plan. Quoting the Messiah, the Psalmist says, "A body you prepared for me." The focus is now on one person, who is the Christ.

Christ Came to do the Father's Will

7 ¶ Then I said, 'Here I am—it is written about me in the scroll—I have come to do your will, O God.'"

The body was prepared but needed to be sacrificed. Continuing to quote from the 40th Psalm, the author demonstrates that the Messiah would be willing to do God's bidding. The Messiah is the one the psalmist wrote about, and he states, "I have come to do your will O God." The Messiah would be obedient to God, even to the point of giving his life.

The Accomplishments of the Lamb of God (10:8-18)

8 First he said, "Sacrifices and offerings, burnt offerings and sin offerings you did not desire, nor were you pleased with them" (although the law required them to be made). 9 Then he said, "Here I am, I have come to do your will." He sets aside the first to establish the second. 10 And by that will, we have been made holy through the sacrifice of the body of Jesus Christ once for all. 11 Day after day every priest stands and performs his religious duties; again and again he offers the same sacrifices, which can never take away sins. 12 But when this priest had offered for all time one sacrifice for sins, he sat down at the right hand of God. 13 Since that time he waits for his enemies to be made his footstool, 14 because by one sacrifice he has made perfect forever those who are being made holy. 15 The Holy Spirit also testifies to us about this. First he says: 16 "This is the covenant I will make with them after that time, says the Lord. I will put my laws in their hearts, and I will write them on their minds." 17 Then he adds: "Their sins and lawless acts I will remember no more." 18 And where these have been forgiven, there is no longer any sacrifice for sin.

Psalm 40 focused on the person of the Messiah and the body prepared for him. It was demonstrated that the Messiah would be obedient to the will of God. With this background established, the author of Hebrews brings his readers towards Jesus. He shows the accomplishments of the Messiah's sacrifice and shows the Hebrews that Jesus is the one true Messiah.

He Set Aside the Sacrificial System

8 First he said, "Sacrifices and offerings, burnt offerings and sin offerings you did not desire, nor were you pleased with them" (although the law required them to be made). 9 Then he said, "here I am, I have come to do your will." he sets aside the first to establish the second.

The old covenant of law and sacrifices was to be set aside at the coming of the Messiah. Repeating his quotes from the 40th Psalm, the author focuses on the body of the Messiah. He makes it clear that the old covenant sacrifices are set aside in favor of the new covenant. The new covenant is wrapped up in one person, the Messiah, who comes to do the will of the Father.

He Made Believers Holy

10 And by that will, we have been made holy through the sacrifice of the body of Jesus Christ once for all. 11 Day after day every priest stands and performs his religious duties; again and again he offers the same sacrifices, which can never take away sins. 12 But when this priest had offered for all time one sacrifice for sins, he sat down at the right hand of God. 13 Since that time he waits for his enemies to be made his footstool, 14 because by one sacrifice he has made perfect forever those who are being made holy.

At this point, Jesus is introduced into the argument. The knowledge of Jesus' death, burial and resurrection was common among the Hebrews. There were eyewitnesses to the resurrection that were still alive and could give testimony. Jesus was the fulfillment of Psalm 40. He had a body prepared for him and willingly sacrificed it on the cross. Paul's writing to the Philippians succinctly presents what Jesus did:

> Who, being in very nature God, did not consider equality with God something to be

grasped, but made himself nothing, taking the very nature of a servant, being made in human likeness. And being found in appearance as a man, he humbled himself and became obedient to death—even death on a cross! (Philippians 2:6-8)

The sacrifice of the body of Jesus has made believers holy once for all. Holiness is the requirement for coming into the presence of God. The sacrificial system could not solve the problem of holiness; however, Jesus' sacrifice did.

There are some strong comparisons and contrasts between these verses and verses one and two of chapter ten. Verse one spoke of the ineffectiveness of, "The same sacrifices repeated endlessly year after year." Verse eleven again picks up the theme of the same sacrifices never being able to take away sin.

Verse two made the argument that, if the sacrifices had been effective, they would have stopped being offered. Verse twelve demonstrates that after the sacrifice of Christ, sacrifices have stopped being offered. This is seen in two ways. First, he is called the one sacrifice for sins for all time. It is one sacrifice and it is for all time. Second, Jesus sat down. Priests never sat down in the temple because their work was never finished. His being seated demonstrates the completion of his work, which was to provide a suitable sacrifice for mankind.

Once again, Jesus is seated at the right hand of God. This is the place of power and authority which is the emphasis of the following verse, which says he is waiting for his enemies to be made his footstool. While Jesus provided the once-for-all sacrifice, the entire created order is not yet as it should be. Enemies such as Satan, demons, unbelievers, sin and death have not yet been put in their appropriate place.

There is a tension between the effective accomplishments of Jesus' death and the way things will eventually pan out. This tension is effectively identified in verse 14. By his sacrifice, Jesus has made believers perfect forever. This has accomplished the very thing that verse one informed readers could not be accomplished through the sacrificial system. This perfection amounts to positional holiness. Through the sacrifice of Jesus, God has declared believers to be holy.

Verse 14 also speaks of believers being made holy. This deals with practical righteousness. Even after the sacrifice of Christ, sin has been allowed to continue in the world. Believers have been declared righteous but continue to sin. The Holy Spirit's work of sanctification is to bring men's actions into line with their position. In other words, he is working to make men holy. This activity will not see its culmination until Jesus returns.

He Put Laws on Believer's Hearts

15 The Holy Spirit also testifies to us about this. First he says:
16 "This is the covenant I will make with them after that time, says the Lord. I will put my laws in their hearts, and I will write them on their minds."

The process by which the Holy Spirit brings men to holiness is to write God's laws on their heart. The old covenant was an external code that dealt with external violations. It said, "Thou shalt not murder." Murderers were found guilty under the law. When Jesus walked the earth, he said that hating one's brother was the equivalent of murder (Matt 5:21-22). No external code could determine whether there was hate in a person's heart. An internal code was needed to accomplish such a task. The new covenant has written God's law on believer's hearts which the Holy Spirit uses to convict of sin, righteousness, and judgment (John 16:7-11).

He Provided Forgiveness

17 Then he adds: "Their sins and lawless acts I will remember no more." 18 And where these have been forgiven, there is no longer any sacrifice for sin.

The sacrifice of Jesus accomplished what the Old Testament sacrifices were incapable of doing. He dealt with the sin problem. The sins of believers are remembered no more. The two goals of a priesthood were accomplished by Jesus. First, believers have been made positionally perfect and can therefore approach God. Second, the problem of sin has been dealt with in that God will no longer remember the believer's sins. Since both these objectives have been met in the sacrifice of Jesus, no other sacrifice will ever be acceptable. The old covenant and its sacrificial system have been set aside to establish the new covenant and the one-time sacrifice of Jesus.

The author of Hebrews previously stated that the old covenant was obsolete and aging and will soon pass away. (Heb 8:13) He now makes it clear that the sacrifice of Jesus is the event that has moved God's plan from the old covenant to the new. Sacrifices would continue until the destruction of the temple in 70 AD. At that time, there would be no doubt that sacrifices had no power to save a person. Those who were saved under the old covenant by faith in the coming Messiah would no longer be able to demonstrate their faith by sacrifices. Having now been enlightened with the knowledge of the effectiveness of Jesus' sacrifice, they must move to the new covenant. They must now believe, not in the coming Messiah, but in the Messiah who has come—Jesus.

Chapter Sixteen

Jesus is a Reason
for Superior Faith   (10:19 to 10:39)

Basis of Faith   (10:19-21)

19 ¶ Therefore, brothers, since we have confidence to enter the Most Holy Place by the blood of Jesus, 20 by a new and living way opened for us through the curtain, that is, his body, 21 and since we have a great priest over the house of God,

The Hebrews who were believing in the coming Messiah had lived their lives walking by faith. Their faith was expressed by confidence in a sacrificial system and the operation of the priesthood. The argument of the book now calls for confidence in a different sacrifice and a different priest.

The Blood of Jesus

19 ¶ Therefore, brothers, since we have confidence to enter the Most Holy Place by the blood of Jesus, 20 by a new and living way opened for us through the curtain, that is, his body,

The author refers to his readers as brothers in order to identify with them in their Hebrew heritage. Using an illustration of the temple, he will enlighten them to the possibility of new-found confidence in going to God.
The Most Holy Place was entered only once a year by the high priest and never without blood. The author informs his

readers that they are now able to enter the Most Holy Place by the blood of Jesus. He is not talking about the earthly tabernacle but rather the heavenly dwelling of God.

Just as a curtain separated the Most Holy Place from the rest of the tabernacle, so also a curtain must be passed through in order to reach the Most Holy Place. He describes this curtain as the body of Jesus. It is through the torn body of Christ that the way to God is opened. This was symbolically demonstrated at the time of Christ's death when the temple veil was ripped from top to bottom. (Matt 27:51) The Most Holy Place could not be entered without blood, but the blood of Jesus was available to all who would draw near to God.

The Priesthood of Jesus

21 and since we have a great priest over the house of God,

The Hebrews were accustomed to the high priest representing them and being the only one that could draw close to God. They were not left without a priest in the new covenant. The new high priest was Jesus. His priesthood and his sacrifice have been major emphases of the entire book to this point. The author, having presented all his arguments, is about to call for action from his readers. He will call them to draw near to God by faith. The basis of that faith is the sacrificial blood of Jesus and his eternal priesthood over the house of God.

Actions of Faith   (10:22-25)

22 let us draw near to God with a sincere heart in full assurance of faith, having our hearts sprinkled to cleanse us from a guilty conscience and having our bodies washed with pure water. 23 Let us hold unswervingly to the hope we profess, for he who promised is faithful. 24 And let us consider how we may spur one another on towards love and good deeds. 25 Let us not give up meeting together, as some are in the habit of doing, but let us encourage one another—and all the more as you see the Day approaching.

The argument in the book now brings the readers to the moment of decision. If Jesus is the Messiah who has come, they must put their faith in him. If Jesus is the basis of their faith, they must take some actions that demonstrate their faith.

Draw Near to God in Faith

22 let us draw near to God with a sincere heart in full assurance of faith, having our hearts sprinkled to cleanse us from a guilty conscience and having our bodies washed with pure water.

The first exhortation deals with the very goals of a priestly system, that is, drawing near to God and dealing with the problem of sin. The Hebrews are exhorted, on the basis of faith in Jesus, to draw near to God. The problem of their lack of holiness has been solved by the once-for-all sacrifice of Jesus. They are able to do this without a guilty conscience because their sins have been cleansed by the blood of Jesus.

Their sincerity of heart must reflect faith in Jesus only. It cannot be a double-minded faith that holds on to the old covenant, while adding Jesus to it. Faith in Jesus will give them full assurance that they are able to enter into God's presence.

Two activities that went on in the temple were the sprinkling of the blood of the sacrifice on those things that needed to be cleansed and the ceremonial washings done by the priests. Alluding to these activities, the author informs his readers that their very hearts have been cleansed by the sprinkling of the blood of Jesus upon them. They have also had their bodies washed with pure water. Jesus, during his lifetime, stood at the temple and declared himself to be living water (John 7:37). With cleansed hearts and bodies, the Hebrews were now free of the guilt of sin and able to draw near to God.

Hold Unswervingly to Hope

23 Let us hold unswervingly to the hope we profess, for he who promised is faithful.

Both the writer and his readers have professed a common hope in the plan of God. Prior to Jesus' arrival, the hope that they professed was identical. Both author and reader would have been professing the hope that the Messiah would come soon. They had a common hope in a promise of God. God is faithful. The promise has come to fruition. Now is not the time to abandon hope, rather to put hope in the Lord Jesus.

The argument of Hebrews has drawn a clear path from the promises of the Old Testament to the person of Jesus. The Hebrews must not swerve from that path but continue to profess hope in their faithful God who has delivered what he promised: the Messiah—Jesus.

Exhort One Another in Love

24 And let us consider how we may spur one another on towards love and good deeds. 25 Let us not give up meeting together, as some are in the habit of doing, but let us encourage one another—and all the more as you see the Day approaching.

Once the Hebrews have drawn near to God and professed faith and hope in Jesus, they are now exhorted to be a demonstration to the community of faith. They are to love one another, do good deeds for one another and encourage each other to do the same. The exhortation to meet together, combined with the fact that some were not doing it, shows a loss of hope on their part. The author encourages them to meet together and be an encouragement to one another. This encouragement would be in the area of increasing their confidence about Jesus being the Messiah. There was a day coming soon when that encouragement would be needed.

The encouragement was needed all the more as the Hebrews would see the day approaching. While some refer to this day as the second coming of the Lord, I think that is unlikely. This book was written to first-century Hebrews who would see a significant day in their lifetime. The day I believe is being spoken of is the day the Romans destroyed the temple.

The author had already made the statement that the old covenant was obsolete and aging and would soon disappear (Heb 8:13). The old covenant effectively disappeared in 70 AD when the temple and its sacrificial system were destroyed. At the time of his writing the author said that event would soon happen. That is most likely the day to which he was referring in this section.

This fits the context very well, inasmuch as the Hebrews would need much encouragement when their sacrificial system under the old covenant was destroyed. They would need to be encouraged that the sacrifice of Jesus was sufficient and the old covenant system was unnecessary and had been set aside.

Notice, in all of these exhortations the author has used the words "we" and "us." After saying, "Let us encourage one another" he then changes from "we" to "you." He says,

223

"And all the more as you see the day approaching." It is as if he has some information about the coming day and they will eventually see it. This adds to the argument that the day is likely the destruction of the temple.

Rejection of Faith   (10:26-31)

26 If we deliberately keep on sinning after we have received the knowledge of the truth, no sacrifice for sins is left, 27 but only a fearful expectation of judgment and of raging fire that will consume the enemies of God. 28 Anyone who rejected the law of Moses died without mercy on the testimony of two or three witnesses. 29 How much more severely do you think a man deserves to be punished who has trampled the Son of God under foot, who has treated as an unholy thing the blood of the covenant that sanctified him, and who has insulted the Spirit of grace? 30 For we know him who said, "It is mine to avenge; I will repay," and again, "The Lord will judge his people." 31 It is a dreadful thing to fall into the hands of the living God.

Throughout the book of Hebrews there are several stern warnings to the people. The warnings particularly concern the sin of unbelief. In chapter two, verse one, the people were told to pay careful attention to what they had heard. In chapter three, verse seven, they were told not to harden their hearts. In chapter three, verses eighteen and nineteen, the sins of disobedience and unbelief were equated. In other words, not to believe the message would be the equivalent of being disobedient. In chapter six, verse four, they were warned not to fall away, that is, to depart from the truth.

This next warning follows the same pattern in that it deals with the sin of unbelief.

Rejection of Truth

26 If we deliberately keep on sinning after we have received the knowledge of the truth, no sacrifice for sins is left, 27 but only a fearful expectation of judgment and of raging fire that will consume the enemies of God.

The phrase "deliberately keep on sinning" implies something that is done voluntarily of one's own accord. This voluntary sin became a problem only after the Hebrews had "received the knowledge of the truth." Once they had sufficient knowledge of Jesus to make a right decision about his being the Messiah, they were expected to make the right decision. To know the truth and yet decide not to believe in Jesus was a willful sin.

On the other hand, perhaps there were Hebrews alive at the time who did not have the knowledge of Jesus. They, having been saved under the old covenant by faith in the coming Messiah, were not deliberately committing the sin of unbelief. Once, however, they read the letter to the Hebrews and understood its argument, they were at the point of decision. If they decided to reject Jesus, there was no other sacrifice that would be effective to save them.

Chapter ten, verse four, had already concluded that, "It is impossible for the blood of bulls and goats to take away sins." Since that is the case, failure to put their faith in Jesus' sacrifice, meant that no sacrifice for sins was available.

The result of the sin of unbelief would be judgment. This judgment is described as raging fire to consume the enemies of God. The author is speaking of the eternal judgment of hell and the lake of fire.

Rejection of the Son

28 Anyone who rejected the law of Moses died without mercy on the testimony of two or three witnesses. 29 How much more severely do you think a man deserves to be punished who has trampled the Son of God under foot, who has treated as an unholy thing the blood of the covenant that sanctified him, and who has insulted the Spirit of grace? 30 For we know him who said, "It is mine to avenge; I will repay," and again, "The Lord will judge his people." 31 It is a dreadful thing to fall into the hands of the living God.

Rejecting the truth meant rejecting Jesus as the Son of God. The author uses an argument from the lesser to the greater to demonstrate the severity of rejecting the Son. He reminds them that rejecting the Law of Moses resulted in death. They certainly understood this. After all, they were saved under the old covenant by faith in the promises of God, communicated by Moses, that a Messiah was to come.

If death resulted from rejecting Moses, how much more should the punishment be for someone who rejects the Son of God. The author describes the effect of rejecting the Son with three terms: trampling the Son of God underfoot; treating as an unholy thing the blood of the covenant; and insulting the Spirit of grace.

Rejecting Jesus, as the Messiah who was to come, would mean that they concluded he was a false Messiah. If that were the case, they would conclude he deserved to die or be trampled underfoot. They would also conclude that his blood was not acceptable. The term "blood of the covenant that sanctified him" refers to Jesus. It was his blood that set him apart (sanctified). His blood was different from any other blood that had ever been brought into the Holy of Holies. His blood was holy. To reject Jesus would be to conclude that his blood was an unholy thing.

God's sacrifice of his Son on the cross was the greatest act of mercy and grace ever performed. To reject that sacrifice would be to insult the Spirit of grace.

The result of rejecting the Son is to be judged by God. God's vengeance does not imply vindictiveness; rather it is the administration of justice. God is just, and rejection of his Son will result in the most dreadful of punishments.

Continuing in Faith (10:32-39)

32 Remember those earlier days after you had received the light, when you stood your ground in a great contest in the face of suffering. 33 Sometimes you were publicly exposed to insult and persecution; at other times you stood side by side with those who were so treated. 34 You sympathized with those in prison and joyfully accepted the confiscation of your property, because you knew that you yourselves had better and lasting possessions. 35 So do not throw away your confidence; it will be richly rewarded. 36 You need to persevere so that when you have done the will of God, you will receive what he has promised. 37 For in just a very little while, "He who is coming will come and will not delay. 38 But my righteous one will live by faith. And if he shrinks back, I will not be pleased with him." 39 But we are not of those who shrink back and are destroyed, but of those who believe and are saved.

Both the old covenant and the new covenant were faith systems. The first required faith in the Messiah who was to come. The second required faith in the Messiah who had come, that is, Jesus. In the next three verses, the author compliments the Hebrews on their earlier faith. Following that, he exhorts them to continue in faith and to believe God's program and be saved.

An Earlier Faith

32 Remember those earlier days after you had received the light, when you stood your ground in a great contest in the face

227

of suffering. 33 Sometimes you were publicly exposed to insult and persecution; at other times you stood side by side with those who were so treated. 34 You sympathized with those in prison and joyfully accepted the confiscation of your property, because you knew that you yourselves had better and lasting possessions.

The Hebrew audience had been people of faith before the death, burial and resurrection of Christ. The term "earlier days" talks about their faith struggle under the old covenant before they became aware of Jesus' arrival. Acts 18, verse 2, reports Jewish persecution under Claudius who was the Emperor of the Roman Empire from 41 AD to 54 AD. Persecution under Claudius was against Jews. His edict was for all Jews to leave Rome.

The term "received the light" immediately causes some modern readers to infer conversion and faith in Jesus. While that is true of our current day, it is not necessarily the understanding of the original audience. Prior to the coming of Jesus, receiving the light could certainly have meant coming to faith in the coming Messiah under the old covenant. In describing the coming of the Messiah, Simeon states he is:

> a light for revelation to the Gentiles and for
> glory to your people Israel. (Luke 2:32)

Notice the distinction: the arrival of Jesus brings light to the Gentiles but is the glory of the Hebrews. Those who had already been enlightened (that is the Hebrews) could now see the fulfillment of their faith, that is, Jesus, the glory of Israel.

The earlier faith of the Hebrews was not without a price. The Jews, even before Jesus came, were under the stern hand of the Roman government. Public insult, persecution, and mistreatment were commonplace in the history of the

Jews, including during the time of the writing of Hebrews. Persecutions under Claudius (41 AD - 54 AD) and under Nero (54 AD - 68 AD) are well documented. In fact Jewish persecution became so intolerable that in 66 AD the Jews revolted against the Roman Empire. Throughout their decades of persecution, the Jews stood against their persecutors because the knew they had better and lasting possessions. They had the promises of God to the patriarchs. Their better and lasting possessions included a land that would be theirs forever, a seed who would be the Messianic King, and blessings of God that would be eternal. Their earlier faith had wonderful promises, but with it came persecution.

Believing Faith

35 So do not throw away your confidence; it will be richly rewarded. 36 You need to persevere so that when you have done the will of God, you will receive what he has promised. 37 For in just a very little while, "He who is coming will come and will not delay. 38 But my righteous one will live by faith. And if he shrinks back, I will not be pleased with him." 39 But we are not of those who shrink back and are destroyed, but of those who believe and are saved.

The Hebrews had great confidence in the promises under the old covenant. The author exhorts them not to throw that confidence away. He tells them to do the will of God and they will receive what he has promised. John tells us what it is to do the will of God:

> For my Father's will is that everyone who looks to the Son and believes in him shall have eternal life, and I will raise him up at the last day." (John 6:40)

God's will for the Hebrews was that they would confidently persevere in faith by placing that faith in Jesus the Messiah who had come.

The author now quotes from the prophet Habakkuk. Habakkuk's prophecy was given to the Israelites to encourage them at the time of an impending invasion by the Babylonians. It was understood by the Jews as an end-time prophecy. The author applies it to the Messiah and to the person of Jesus. The original wording of the Greek says:

> For yet a very little (while) the coming (one)
> will come and will not delay.

The first-century Hebrews were looking for the one who was to come, or the "coming one." They were looking for him to establish the Messianic kingdom. Jesus was a disappointment to many in that he did not establish the kingdom at his coming. The author uses the Habakkuk quote to restore the people's hope for a coming Messianic kingdom. He tells them the "coming one," that is, Jesus, will come. In essence, he is saying he will come again to establish the kingdom.

This is consistent with his teaching in chapter nine. In verse 26, he made the point that the Messiah, "has appeared once for all at the end of the ages to do away with sin by the sacrifice of himself." In verse 28 he says that the Messiah, "will appear a second time not to bear sin but to bring salvation to those who are waiting for him." The one who is the Messiah who has come is also the Messiah who will come again and will not delay.

Still quoting from Habakkuk, the author reminds his audience to live by faith. They have lived a life of faith under the old covenant and must not shrink back because of this new revelation that Jesus is the one who has come. They must move ahead and believe in Jesus or God will not be pleased.

The author inspires confidence by suggesting that the Hebrews are not those who will shrink back, but those who will believe and be saved. It is a clear call to put their belief in Jesus the Messiah who has come and who will come again. The Hebrews' salvation depends on this decision. If they shrink back from their walk of faith, they will be destroyed. They must continue in their faith by believing that God's plan included Jesus as his Son who is the Messiah who was to come.

Chapter Seventeen

Jesus is a Reason
for Superior Saints   (11:1 to 11:40)

The Faith of
the Pre-Flood Ancients   (11:1-7)

1 ¶ Now faith is being sure of what we hope for and certain of what we do not see. 2 This is what the ancients were commended for. 3 By faith we understand that the universe was formed at God's command, so that what is seen was not made out of what was visible. 4 ¶ By faith Abel offered God a better sacrifice than Cain did. By faith he was commended as a righteous man, when God spoke well of his offerings. And by faith he still speaks, even though he is dead. 5 By faith Enoch was taken from this life, so that he did not experience death; he could not be found, because God had taken him away. For before he was taken, he was commended as one who pleased God. 6 And without faith it is impossible to please God, because anyone who comes to him must believe that he exists and that he rewards those who earnestly seek him. 7 By faith Noah, when warned about things not yet seen, in holy fear built an ark to save his family. By his faith he condemned the world and became heir of the righteousness that comes by faith.

The author just inspired his readers with the statement that they are not of those who shrink back and are destroyed but of those who believe and are saved. He now takes the next 40 verses to give examples of those who walked by faith in the most difficult situations. This chapter is often called "the honor roll of faith." The main emphasis of the chapter is believing God, not the actions of the individuals. They are not commended for their activity but rather for their belief. Their activity was only the logical expression of their strong faith.

Certainty of Faith

1 ¶ Now faith is being sure of what we hope for and certain of what we do not see. 2 This is what the ancients were commended for. 3 By faith we understand that the universe was formed at God's command, so that what is seen was not made out of what was visible.

Inasmuch as this entire chapter concentrates on men of faith, it is important to understand what faith is. Faith is an attitude of certainty towards those things that have not yet been made visible. Belief in a promise that is future can only be established by faith. One's faith is only as sure as the object of that faith. When the object of faith is the promises of God, one can be certain of what one does not see.

The examples that follow demonstrate that the ancients were commended for this kind of faith. When examining these Old Testament accounts, the great achievements of those involved are not the point. The focus is the faith that resulted in the works.

The starting point of any faith is to believe that there is a God who created the universe. No one was around to bear witness to the creation, but God's Word says he created the world in six days. This must be accepted by faith. Only through faith can one be certain of what is not seen. One will be commended for believing in God's creation of the universe.

On the other hand, those who would argue for evolution have demonstrated that they do not put their faith in the truth of God's Word. Inasmuch as God's Word says he created the heavens and the earth, to believe anything else is not faith, but foolishness.

By Faith the Proper Sacrifice was Offered

4 ¶ By faith Abel offered God a better sacrifice than Cain did. By faith he was commended as a righteous man, when God spoke well of his offerings. And by faith he still speaks, even though he is dead.

Abel's and Cain's sacrifices represent the early worship of God recorded in the book of Genesis:

> In the course of time Cain brought some of the fruits of the soil as an offering to the LORD. But Abel brought fat portions from some of the firstborn of his flock. The LORD looked with favor on Abel and his offering, but on Cain and his offering he did not look with favor. So Cain was very angry, and his face was downcast. (Gen 4:3-5)

There are three things implied in the text that deal with worship. Cain and Abel brought their offerings to a specific place so there must have been a designated place for worship. It is likely that this place was at the entrance to the Garden of Eden. In the previous chapter of Genesis, mankind had been expelled from the garden and two cherubim placed on the east side to guard the entrance. Inasmuch as this was as close as mankind could get to the place where they used to dwell with God, it is likely that an altar was established there. This may have been a forerunner to the Mercy Seat, which was the place of sacrifice in the tabernacle. It was made with two golden cherubim above it.

Not only was there a place of worship, but there was a

specific time of worship. The expression, "in the course of time" means literally "at the end of days." In the previous chapters of Genesis the only cycle of days that has been mentioned is the seven days of creation. This week long cycle was very likely the cycle that mankind has followed ever since. The end of days is likely the last day of the week. This could possibly be an early reference to mankind honoring the Sabbath day.

The text also implies that there was a specific way to worship. It is uncertain why Cain's offering was not accepted and Abel's was. Two possibilities exist. The first is the distinction between Cain bringing "some of the fruits" as opposed to Abel bringing the "firstborn of his flock." The issue becomes, "Why did Cain not bring firstfruits?" While this distinction is a possibility, the answer that is more consistent with the entire flow of Scripture deals with the shedding of blood.

It is more likely that God had instructed Cain and Abel to bring a blood sacrifice. Throughout Scripture, the blood sacrifice is of great importance. Eventually the writer to Hebrews would remind his readers that, without the shedding of blood, there is no forgiveness. (Heb 9:22)

Abel's offering was offered by faith, that is, he believed God and did what he was told. Cain, on the other hand, was willing to worship God but on his own terms. He did not believe God but rather brought an offering of his own design. Mankind must not only believe that there is a God but must believe God. Faith is trusting God and believing that his way is right. Worship outside of the manner expressed by God is disobedience. Abel was commended as a righteous man because his sacrifice demonstrated that he believed God.

Hebrews instructs that by faith Abel still speaks even though he is dead. In the Genesis account, Abel's blood is said to cry out from the ground:

The LORD said, "What have you done? Listen! Your brother's blood cries out to me from the ground. Now you are under a curse and driven from the ground, which opened its mouth to receive your brother's blood from your hand. When you work the ground, it will no longer yield its crops for you. You will be a restless wanderer on the earth." (Gen 4:10-12)

Abel's blood cried out to God. This is consistent with the later teaching of Moses as recorded in the book of Numbers:

Do not pollute the land where you are. Bloodshed pollutes the land, and atonement cannot be made for the land on which blood has been shed, except by the blood of the one who shed it. (Num 35:33)

The first person Abel's blood spoke to was God as it cried out for vengeance. It also spoke to Cain, in that it was a constant reminder of his evil deed. Abel's blood still speaks today reminding mankind that he must come to God by faith, in obedience, and that sin will be punished.

By Faith a Rapture Took Place

5 By faith Enoch was taken from this life, so that he did not experience death; he could not be found, because God had taken him away. For before he was taken, he was commended as one who pleased God. 6 And without faith it is impossible to please God, because anyone who comes to him must believe that he exists and that he rewards those who earnestly seek him.

Enoch walked so closely with God that he did not experience death but was taken right into heaven. It is uncertain why Enoch experienced this particular phenomenon. He is, however, an effective picture of believers who will be raptured when the Lord returns. The apostle Paul writes:

> After that, we who are still alive and are left will be caught up together with them in the clouds to meet the Lord in the air. And so we will be with the Lord forever. (1 Thess 4:17)

Enoch's rapture was a result of his pleasing God. There are a number of things in the text that indicate how he pleased God. First of all, he believed that God exists. This is the first step of faith that anyone can take. Believing in the existence of God alone is not sufficient to save a person but if it is a sincere conviction, it is very likely it will lead to saving faith. Belief in God means belief in the God of Scripture, not simply in some god of man's own design.

Enoch did not only believe God existed but he came to God. He recognized God as a personal, loving, gracious God and desired to be with him.

Enoch is also mentioned in the book of Jude:

> Enoch, the seventh from Adam, prophesied about these men: "See, the Lord is coming with thousands upon thousands of his holy ones to judge everyone, and to convict all the ungodly of all the ungodly acts they have done in the ungodly way, and of all the harsh words ungodly sinners have spoken against him." (Jude 1:14-15)

It is evident that Enoch was a preacher of righteousness. He clearly brought a message of coming judgment to the world in which he lived.

It was not Enoch's works that allowed him to be translated into heaven, rather his faith. He believed in God and he believed God.

By Faith Eight Escaped the Flood

7 By faith Noah, when warned about things not yet seen, in holy fear built an ark to save his family. By his faith he condemned the world and became heir of the righteousness that comes by faith.

Noah built the ark in holy fear or reverence for God. This is a statement that he believed all that God said. God said some incredible things.

> So God said to Noah, "I am going to put an end to all people, for the earth is filled with violence because of them. I am surely going to destroy both them and the earth. So make yourself an ark of cypress wood; make rooms in it and coat it with pitch inside and out. This is how you are to build it: The ark is to be 450 feet long, 75 feet wide and 45 feet high. Make a roof for it and finish the ark to within 18 inches of the top. Put a door in the side of the ark and make lower, middle and upper decks. I am going to bring floodwaters on the earth to destroy all life under the heavens, every creature that has the breath of life in it. Everything on earth will perish. (Gen 6:13-17)

Noah lived nowhere near water, but he nonetheless believed that God would bring a flood. His holy fear came from his belief that God would destroy all life under the heavens.

Noah not only built the ark, but he was also called to preach a message of judgment as he built. As with Enoch, one must look to the New Testament to discover that Noah was "a preacher of righteousness" (2 Peter 2:5). Noah's preaching was a warning to the world and the condemnation of it.

Noah was characterized as a righteous man because he believed God. He was not righteous because of his skills in ark building. He was declared righteous because he believed the message God gave him.

The Faith of
the Patriarchs   (11:8-22)

8 By faith Abraham, when called to go to a place he would later receive as his inheritance, obeyed and went, even though he did not know where he was going. 9 By faith he made his home in the promised land like a stranger in a foreign country; he lived in tents, as did Isaac and Jacob, who were heirs with him of the same promise. 10 For he was looking forward to the city with foundations, whose architect and builder is God. 11 By faith Abraham, even though he was past age—and Sarah herself was barren—was enabled to become a father because he considered him faithful who had made the promise. 12 And so from this one man, and he as good as dead, came descendants as numerous as the stars in the sky and as countless as the sand on the seashore. 13 All these people were still living by faith when they died. They did not receive the things promised; they only saw them and welcomed them from a distance. And they admitted that they were aliens and strangers on earth. 14 People who say such things show that they are looking for a country of their own. 15 If they had been thinking of the country they had left, they would have had opportunity to return. 16

Instead, they were longing for a better country—a heavenly one. Therefore God is not ashamed to be called their God, for he has prepared a city for them. 17 By faith Abraham, when God tested him, offered Isaac as a sacrifice. He who had received the promises was about to sacrifice his one and only son, 18 even though God had said to him, "It is through Isaac that your offspring will be reckoned." 19 Abraham reasoned that God could raise the dead, and figuratively speaking, he did receive Isaac back from death. 20 By faith Isaac blessed Jacob and Esau in regard to their future. 21 By faith Jacob, when he was dying, blessed each of Joseph's sons, and worshipped as he leaned on the top of his staff. 22 By faith Joseph, when his end was near, spoke about the exodus of the Israelites from Egypt and gave instructions about his bones.

The text of Hebrews moves from the pre-flood saints to those patriarchs who lived after the flood. Beginning with Abraham, the focus of redemptive history is on one family that will become a great nation. Four generations are singled out for commendation as to their faith. They are: Abraham, Isaac, Jacob and Joseph. Each of them believed the promises of God.

By Faith Difficult Commands were Obeyed

8 By faith Abraham, when called to go to a place he would later receive as his inheritance, obeyed and went, even though he did not know where he was going. 9 By faith he made his home in the promised land like a stranger in a foreign country; he lived in tents, as did Isaac and Jacob, who were heirs with him of the same promise. 10 For he was looking forward to the city with foundations, whose architect and builder is God.

The promises given to Abraham, referred to as the Abrahamic covenant, are recorded in Genesis chapter 12:

The LORD had said to Abram, "Leave your country, your people and your father's household and go to the land I will show you. "I will make you into a great nation and I will bless you; I will make your name great, and you will be a blessing. I will bless those who bless you, and whoever curses you I will curse; and all peoples on earth will be blessed through you."(Gen 12:1-3)

Abraham was promised land, seed and blessing. He did not know where this land was, but he believed God and went his way. Even when arriving at the so-called promised land, he never owned it during his lifetime. Instead, he and his descendants lived in temporary dwellings as strangers in a foreign land. The promise of land was not fulfilled during Abraham's lifetime.

Abraham's faith continued throughout his lifetime because he understood that there was a heavenly city to look forward to. Whether Abraham received land here on this earth was not important. In his walk of faith, he believed that God had something greater planned for all eternity. Abraham believed God and obeyed his commands wherever they led him.

By Faith a Barren Womb Gave Birth

11 By faith Abraham, even though he was past age—and Sarah herself was barren—was enabled to become a father because he considered him faithful who had made the promise. 12 And so from this one man, and he as good as dead, came descendants as numerous as the stars in the sky and as countless as the sand on the seashore. 13 All these people were still living by faith when they died. They did not receive the things promised; they only saw them and welcomed them from a distance. And they admitted that they were aliens and strangers on earth. 14 People who say such things show that they are looking for a country of their own. 15 If they had been thinking of the country they had left, they would have had opportunity to return. 16 Instead, they were longing for a better country—a heavenly one. Therefore God is not ashamed to be called their God, for he has prepared a city for them.

The promise to Abraham not only included land but also an heir. The promise is expounded in Genesis 15:

Then the word of the LORD came to him: "This man will not be your heir, but a son coming from your own body will be your heir." He took him outside and said, "Look up at the heavens and count the stars—if indeed you can count them." Then he said to him, "So shall your offspring be." Abram believed the LORD, and he credited it to him as righteousness.(Gen 15:4-6)

This was an amazing promise made to an old man with a barren wife. There was nothing Abraham could do to make this promise come to pass. He had to trust God. The text says Abraham believed the Lord and it was credited to him as righteousness. The way to righteousness is always by faith. In his New Testament discussion of righteousness, Paul declares to the Romans:

But now a righteousness from God, apart from law, has been made known, to which the law and the Prophets testify. This righteousness from God comes through faith in Jesus Christ to all who believe. There is no difference for all have sinned and fall short of the glory of God. (Rom 3:21-23)

Abraham believed that God would send him a son and from him would come descendants as numerous as the stars of the sky. God indeed did send him Isaac and millions have descended from him. More importantly, the seed of Abraham eventually resulted in the Messiah:

> The promises were spoken to Abraham and to his seed. The Scripture does not say "and to seeds," meaning many people, but "and to your seed," meaning one person, who is Christ. (Gal 3:16)

All those who have put their faith in Jesus, the Messiah, are the spiritual children of Abraham. (Gal 3:29)

Abraham, Sarah, Isaac and Jacob did not experience the fulfillment of God's promises to any great extent. They nonetheless believed God and were looking ahead to a heavenly fulfillment of God's promise. They did not have to see to believe. They believed God and walked in obedience to him.

By Faith the Sacrifice was Offered

17 By faith Abraham, when God tested him, offered Isaac as a sacrifice. He who had received the promises was about to sacrifice his one and only son, 18 even though God had said to him, "It is through Isaac that your offspring will be reckoned." 19 Abraham reasoned that God could raise the dead, and figuratively speaking, he did receive Isaac back from death.

Abraham's faith was severely tested when God asked him to sacrifice Isaac, the promised heir. If Isaac was killed, the promise of descendants as numerous as the stars of the

sky could not be fulfilled. Abraham could not figure out
what God was doing by making such a request. He nonetheless knew that he could believe God. He could even believe
God to raise the dead in order to keep his promise.

Abraham willingly took his son to Mount Moriah and
prepared to sacrifice him on an altar. The Lord intervened at
the last moment and provided a ram as a substitute sacrifice.
This is a beautiful picture of the ultimate sacrifice of the
Son of God at Mount Calvary. Mount Moriah and Mount
Calvary are in the same area, as is also the temple mount on
which Solomon would build a temple where sacrifices
would be made in obedience to the law of Moses.

Abraham's willingness to sacrifice Isaac and the entire
sacrificial system of the Mosaic law pointed to the ultimate
sacrifice of Jesus at Calvary. The same faith in God was
required in Abraham's day, in the old covenant economy,
and under the new covenant, as well.

By Faith Great Predictions were Made

*20 By faith Isaac blessed Jacob and Esau in regard to their
future. 21 By faith Jacob, when he was dying, blessed each of
Joseph's sons, and worshipped as he leaned on the top of his
staff. 22 By faith Joseph, when his end was near, spoke about
the exodus of the Israelites from Egypt and gave instructions
about his bones.*

In Isaac's blessings of Jacob and Esau he demonstrated
his faith in the promises of God. In Genesis 28 a blessing of
Jacob is recorded.

> So Isaac called for Jacob and blessed him
> and commanded him: "Do not marry a
> Canaanite woman. Go at once to Paddan
> Aram, to the house of your mother's father

245

> Bethuel. Take a wife for yourself there, from among the daughters of Laban, your mother's brother. May God Almighty bless you and make you fruitful and increase your numbers until you become a community of peoples. May he give you and your descendants the blessing given to Abraham, so that you may take possession of the land where you now live as an alien, the land God gave to Abraham."(Gen 28:1-4)

This blessing showed that Isaac was still believing the promises of God, even as he neared death.

Likewise, when Jacob was nearing his death, his blessing of Joseph's children demonstrated his faith:

> "I am with you and will watch over you wherever you go, and I will bring you back to this land. I will not leave you until I have done what I have promised you." When Jacob awoke from his sleep, he thought, "Surely the LORD is in this place, and I was not aware of it." (Gen 48:15-16)

Jacob also blessed all of his children. His blessing to Judah is a prediction of the Messiah to come.

> The sceptre will not depart from Judah, nor the ruler's staff from between his feet, until he comes to whom it belongs and the obedience of the nations is his. (Gen 49:10)

Jacob's blessings demonstrate a continuing belief in God even at the time of his death.

Similarly, Joseph demonstrated his continuing belief at

the time of his death:

> Then Joseph said to his brothers, "I am about to die. But God will surely come to your aid and take you up out of this land to the land he promised on oath to Abraham, Isaac and Jacob."
> And Joseph made the sons of Israel swear an oath and said, "God will surely come to your aid, and then you must carry my bones up from this place."(Gen 50:24-25)

There were many commendable achievements in Joseph's life that did not get mentioned in this "honor roll of faith." The event that gets singled out is his giving instructions about his bones. The reason is that this demonstrates his absolute faith in the promises of God. He was sure that the land, promised to Abraham, Isaac and Jacob, would eventually be in the hands of their descendants. Giving instructions to bring his bones to the promised land demonstrated the sincerity of his faith.

All of these patriarchs believed God, and that was the source of their righteousness.

The Faith of the Exodus Saints   (11:23-31)

23 By faith Moses' parents hid him for three months after he was born, because they saw he was no ordinary child, and they were not afraid of the king's edict. 24 By faith Moses, when he had grown up, refused to be known as the son of Pharaoh's daughter. 25 He chose to be ill-treated along with the people of God rather than to enjoy the pleasures of sin for a short time. 26 He regarded disgrace for the sake of Christ as of greater value than the treasures of Egypt, because he was looking ahead to his reward. 27 By faith he left Egypt, not fearing the

247

king's anger; he persevered because he saw him who is invisible. 28 By faith he kept the Passover and the sprinkling of blood, so that the destroyer of the firstborn would not touch the firstborn of Israel. 29 By faith the people passed through the Red Sea as on dry land; but when the Egyptians tried to do so, they were drowned. 30 By faith the walls of Jericho fell, after the people had marched around them for seven days. 31 By faith the prostitute Rahab, because she welcomed the spies, was not killed with those who were disobedient.

The honor roll of faith moves to the time of the Exodus. It includes faith lessons from the birth of Moses, the escape from Egypt and the ultimate entrance into the promised land. Throughout that time, God's leaders were asked to walk by faith. They responded by believing God.

By Faith a Babe was Hidden for Three Months

23 By faith Moses' parents hid him for three months after he was born, because they saw he was no ordinary child, and they were not afraid of the king's edict.

Moses' parents somehow perceived that Moses was no ordinary child. This is indicative that they understood God had a special plan for this child. They risked their lives to protect the child, not simply because they loved him, but because they had faith, which implies they were following God's plan. They were not afraid of the king's edict because they believed God.

They believed God not only as they hid the child for several months, but also when they placed him in a basket and allowed him to be discovered by Pharaoh's daughter.

By Faith a Nation was Delivered from Slavery

24 By faith Moses, when he had grown up, refused to be known as the son of Pharaoh's daughter. 25 He chose to be ill-treated along with the people of God rather than to enjoy the pleasures of sin for a short time. 26 He regarded disgrace for the sake of Christ as of greater value than the treasures of Egypt, because he was looking ahead to his reward. 27 By faith he left Egypt, not fearing the king's anger; he persevered because he saw him who is invisible. 28 By faith he kept the Passover and the sprinkling of blood, so that the destroyer of the firstborn would not touch the firstborn of Israel. 29 By faith the people passed through the Red Sea as on dry land; but when the Egyptians tried to do so, they were drowned.

Moses grew up in Pharaoh's palace. He was enjoying the good life. When he was grown, he had a choice whether to be know as Pharaoh's son or identify himself with the Israelite slaves. He believed God was calling him to be the deliverer of his people.

Moses chose to believe God for several reasons given in the text. First, the pleasures of living in the palace were sinful and of short duration. By faith Moses rejected those pleasures.

Second, he regarded disgrace for the sake of Christ as of greater value than the treasures of Egypt. The use of the term "Christ" demonstrates that Moses fully understood the concept of the Messiah. The premise of the book of Hebrews is that the Hebrew believers were saved under the old covenant by faith in the coming Messiah and now had to transfer their faith to Jesus, the Messiah who had come. Moses being disgraced for the sake of Christ is a clear example of an Old Testament saint having faith in the Messiah who was to come. Moses acknowledged that faith in the Messiah was more important than his earthly enjoyment.

Third, Moses believed God because he was looking forward to his reward. Just as Abraham and the patriarchs looked ahead to a heavenly city, so also Moses had a heavenly perspective on his life.

Fourth, he persevered because he saw him who is invisible. Moses had an encounter with God at the burning bush. It is likely that this encounter was with the second person of the trinity, God's Son, whom we know as Jesus. Moses believed all that God had promised.

Moses demonstrated his belief in God and his promises by the things he did. When God was destroying the firstborn of Egypt, Moses trusted him not to destroy the firstborn of Israel and demonstrated his trust by sprinkling blood on the door posts. This simple step of faith demonstrated that he believed and trusted God.

Likewise, when he encountered the Red Sea, he believed God, and the people crossed on dry land. Moses achieved nothing in his own right. He is in the faith hall of fame simply because he believed God.

By Faith a City was Shouted Down

30 By faith the walls of Jericho fell, after the people had marched around them for seven days. 31 By faith the prostitute Rahab, because she welcomed the spies, was not killed with those who were disobedient.

The fall of the walls of Jericho is used to illustrate two significant acts of faith. First, Joshua demonstrated his faith by instructing the Israelites to march around the walls for seven days. There would be no reason to believe that such action would cause these enormous walls to fall. One had simply to believe God or else there would be no compulsion to act in what appeared to be such a foolish manner. Of course, Joshua's faith paid off and the walls fell.

The faith of Rahab is also mentioned in relation to Jericho's fall. This Gentile women, living a life as a prostitute, was faced with a decision. She had information concerning the Israelite spies. She could have given this to the authorities and trusted in the walls of Jericho to protect her. Instead she believed that the God of the Israelites would prevail, so she hid the spies. She demonstrated her faith by believing God and trusting him rather than trusting in the strength of her own nation.

The Faith of
Other Old Testament Saints   (11:32-38)

32 ¶ And what more shall I say? I do not have time to tell about Gideon, Barak, Samson, Jephthah, David, Samuel and the prophets, 33 who through faith conquered kingdoms, administered justice, and gained what was promised; who shut the mouths of lions, 34 quenched the fury of the flames, and escaped the edge of the sword; whose weakness was turned to strength; and who became powerful in battle and routed foreign armies. 35 Women received back their dead, raised to life again. Others were tortured and refused to be released, so that they might gain a better resurrection. 36 Some faced jeers and flogging, while still others were chained and put in prison. 37 They were stoned; they were sawn in two; they were put to death by the sword. They went about in sheepskins and goatskins, destitute, persecuted and ill-treated— 38 the world was not worthy of them. They wandered in deserts and mountains, and in caves and holes in the ground.

The honor roll of faith now brings attention to the periods of the judges, the kings, and the prophets. This section forms a summary of the highlights of that period of Israel's history.

By Faith Many Righteous Acts were Done

32 ¶ And what more shall I say? I do not have time to tell about Gideon, Barak, Samson, Jephthah, David, Samuel and the prophets, 33 who through faith conquered kingdoms, administered justice, and gained what was promised; who shut the mouths of lions, 34 quenched the fury of the flames, and escaped the edge of the sword; whose weakness was turned to strength; and who became powerful in battle and routed foreign armies. 35 Women received back their dead, raised to life again.

The writer of Hebrews enumerates some of the heroes of the faith. Their stories were well known by the Hebrews. A careful analysis of each story would demonstrate belief in God. Their belief in what God promised allowed them to do the incredible and, at times, miraculous things mentioned in this section.

Gideon was a judge and military leader. He was preparing to fight the Midianites and Amalekites with an army of 32,000 men. The Lord intervened and paired Gideon's army down to a mere 300 men on the basis of how they drank water from a spring. The opposing army was described in Judges 7:12, "as numerous as locusts; and their camels were without number, as numerous as the sand on the seashore." Gideon's faith in God secured a victory despite the overwhelming odds against him.

Barak was also a military leader working with Israel's female judge, Deborah. Once again this military leader was charged with facing an overwhelming opponent, the Canaanites. Barak's army of 10,000 had to face a far superior force that included 900 iron chariots besides all the fighting men. Because of the courageous faith of Barak it was reported, "and the Lord routed Sisera and all his chariots and all his army, with the edge of the sword before

Barak." (Judges 4:15)

Samson was also a judge of Israel and his opponent was the Philistines. Throughout Judges 13-16 are accounts of tremendous individual battles of Samson against the Philistines. Certainly Samson had a number of moral short-comings and significant faults but the writer of Hebrews, under the inspiration of the Holy Spirit, nonetheless commends him for his faith. Without faith he could never have achieved the personal victories recorded.

Jephthah was another Judge of Israel. The enemy at that time was the Ammonites. Jephthah's faith and trust in the Lord, as recorded in Judges 11, allowed the people to defeat the Ammonite army.

David was Israel's great king. His military victories were numerous. While his entire life was a walk of faith, one cannot help but single out his battle with Goliath in 1 Samuel 17, as a significant faith challenge. While the Israelite army crowded in fear this young man proclaimed to the giant Goliath, "This day the Lord will deliver you up into my hands, and I will strike you down and remove your head from you." (1 Sam 17:46)

Samuel was the last judge of Israel and was not known as a warrior. The enemy of Israel at that time was its own idolatry and immorality. His walk of faith as recorded in 1 Samuel consisted of prophesying on behalf of God and exhibiting the courage to stand against the tide of idolatry and immorality. Only by faith could he accomplish his task.

The prophets are identified as a group. They, like Samuel, would stand against the evils of their day. They would speak forth God's word before kings and those in authority without fear. Their faith is what made them bold.

The writer of Hebrews lists some of the accomplishments of these men of God which also causes their readers to think of other great men of faith. The expression, "quenched the fury of the flames" could refer to Shadrach,

Meshach, and Abednego who by faith withstood the fiery furnace of King Nebuchadnezzar rather then bow their knee to anyone but God.

The one, "who shut the mouths of lions" was Daniel. He too refused to bow his knee to the Babylonian king, Darius, and found himself thrown into the lion's den. By faith Daniel escaped the certain death that should have been his.

The reference to women receiving back their dead undoubtedly is a reference to Elijah's raising of the child of the Zarephath widow, (1 Kings 17:8-23) and Elisha's raising of the Shunammite women's son. (2 Kings 4:18-37) It was the faith of these prophets and these women that brought the children back to life.

Each of these righteous acts were performed by faith of these Old Testament saints. They serve as a wonderful example of the courageous faith to which all believers are called.

By Faith Many Unrighteous Acts Were Endured

Others were tortured and refused to be released, so that they might gain a better resurrection. 36 Some faced jeers and flogging, while still others were chained and put in prison. 37 They were stoned; they were sawn in two; they were put to death by the sword. They went about in sheepskins and goatskins, destitute, persecuted and ill-treated— 38 the world was not worthy of them. They wandered in deserts and mountains, and in caves and holes in the ground.

Accomplishing great things by faith in God is only half the story. Sometimes individuals are called to endure horrendous sufferings by faith in God. Flogging, stonings, death, persecution, etc., were real evidence that these individuals believed God. They had to have a heavenly perspective. The text concludes that they did what they did "so that they might gain a better resurrection." Clearly, they saw that there was more beyond this life and chose to believe God's promise of something more to come in heaven.

The Faith of
New Testament Saints   (11:39-40)

39 These were all commended for their faith, yet none of them received what had been promised. 40 God had planned something better for us so that only together with us would they be made perfect.

These final verses of Hebrews, chapter eleven, tie together the Old Testament saints with the Hebrews who were now considering the new covenant.

Old Testament Saints did not Receive the Promise

39 These were all commended for their faith, yet none of them received what had been promised.

The promise of a coming Messiah had its roots in Genesis 3:15 where it was prophesied that a seed of the woman would crush Satan's head. The promise was expanded in the covenant with Abraham and was understood to be part of the teaching of the Mosaic Covenant of law. Through the years, Old Testament saints were looking for their land and their Messiah. They were commended for believing God even though they did not receive the promise. Their heavenly perspective allowed them to trust God to fulfill his promise, even though they faced death.

Old and New Made Perfect Together

40 God had planned something better for us so that only

together with us would they be made perfect.

Throughout the book of Hebrews, the author has proven that Jesus is the Messiah who was to come. Jesus, by his sacrifice, made perfect forever those who were being made holy. (Hebrews 10:14) Jesus' sacrifice was not just for the Hebrews who were alive at that time, but his sacrifice was sufficient to make perfect all those believers who had died before the Messiah came. Those who came before the cross were saved by the future sacrifice of the Messiah. Those who came after the cross were saved by looking back at the sacrifice of the Messiah. Together, both groups were made perfect by the one sacrifice.

The first-century Hebrews were a unique generation that had looked forward to the coming of the Messiah and then looked back on the cross. Was Jesus the one? The author of Hebrews has left no doubt that Jesus was the Messiah who had come and the sacrifice that made both Old and New Testament saints perfect forever.

Chapter Eighteen

Jesus is a Reason for
Superior Discipline   (12:1 to 12:16)

Perfecter of Discipline   (12:1-2)

1 ¶ Therefore, since we are surrounded by such a great cloud of witnesses, let us throw off everything that hinders and the sin that so easily entangles, and let us run with perseverance the race marked out for us. 2 Let us fix our eyes on Jesus, the author and perfecter of our faith, who for the joy set before him endured the cross, scorning its shame, and sat down at the right hand of the throne of God.

Hebrews, chapter eleven, consisted of an extensive series of examples of those who had walked by faith. Chapter twelve opens with the word "therefore," which anticipates that the readers will now be instructed in the way of application. In light of all of the theology of chapters one through ten and the examples of chapter eleven, the audience is instructed to applying what they have been taught.

This section deals with discipline. It includes the discipline of a life committed to following the Lord in faith. It also includes the discipline that comes from the Lord to those that are his children.

A Cloud of Witnesses

1 ¶ Therefore, since we are surrounded by such a great cloud of witnesses, let us throw off everything that hinders and the sin that so easily entangles, and let us run with perseverance the race marked out for us.

A life of following the Lord is described as a race. Each individual has a particular race marked out for him. It could be a short sprint or a marathon run. For some it may be a steeple chase with its many hazards along the way, while for others it may be the high hurdles. Regardless of the contest which has been designed, each individual is to run with perseverance.

The great cloud of witnesses is frequently depicted as the individuals of chapter eleven looking down from heaven and witnessing the believers running a race. They are imagined to be cheerleaders of a sort. The context and argument of Hebrews is better served if these witnesses are seen as witnesses "to" the Hebrews as opposed to witnesses "of" the Hebrews. They are not watching the Hebrews, but rather have witnessed to the Hebrews by their acts of faith. They are to be viewed as examples of those who have run the race before them.

There are two problems that believers experience when running the race of life. They are sin and hindrances. Sin, in all of its forms, is to be avoided at all cost.

Things that hinder are those things that keep believers from following God's plan wholeheartedly. Sometimes very good things can become hindrances. In the life of the first-century Hebrew, the old covenant had become a hindrance. It had to be set aside in favor of the new covenant and faith in Jesus.

A Perfect Example

2 Let us fix our eyes on Jesus, the author and perfecter of our faith, who for the joy set before him endured the cross, scorning its shame, and sat down at the right hand of the throne of God.

In setting aside sin and hindrances, including the old covenant, the Hebrews were instructed to fix their eyes on Jesus. He is the one who was the author of their faith, including the requirements of the old covenant.

In Hebrews 10:14 and 11:40 the point was made that the heroes of faith could not be made perfect apart from Jesus. He is the perfecter of faith. The readers are instructed to fix their eyes on Jesus. Having looked at the examples of Old Testament heroes of the faith, they are now told to look at Jesus, the perfect example of faith. The greatest example of Jesus' faith, trust and obedience to the Father is his endurance of the cross of Calvary and the shame that went with it. The NIV and most common translations would indicate that Jesus endured the cross "for" the joy set before him. This gives the impression that he went through the agony of the cross so that he might experience joy on the other side. The problem with this is that Jesus could have had joy and never gone to the cross. He certainly had joy with the Father before coming to earth and could have continued in that joy without enduring the cross.

The word translated "for" is the Greek word "anti" it means "against" or "instead of." Translated in this manner, the expression would say that Jesus "instead of the joy set before him endured the cross." This translation is to be preferred for three reasons. First, it demonstrates the great condescension of Jesus, who left the glory of heaven to be made a little lower than the angels. (Heb 2:9) Second, it is consistent with Jesus being a prophet like unto Moses who gave up the riches of Egypt to be identified with the Israelite slaves. (Heb 11:24) Third, it is consistent with what believers are called to do in following Jesus. They are to set aside the things that would attract them and hinder them and, instead, follow the Lord and do his will wholeheartedly. (Heb 12:1)

Jesus is seated at the right hand of the throne of God.

Jesus' sacrifice on the cross was sufficient to complete his high priestly work. He is now seated in a position of power and authority and is able to make intercession for those who come to him in faith. The faith of the first-century Hebrews was imperfect unless and until they came to Jesus, the perfecter of faith.

Perseverance in Discipline   (12:3-8)

3 Consider him who endured such opposition from sinful men, so that you will not grow weary and lose heart. 4 ¶ In your struggle against sin, you have not yet resisted to the point of shedding your blood. 5 And you have forgotten that word of encouragement that addresses you as sons: "My son, do not make light of the Lord's discipline, and do not lose heart when he rebukes you, 6 because the Lord disciplines those he loves, and he punishes everyone he accepts as a son." 7 Endure hardship as discipline; God is treating you as sons. For what son is not disciplined by his father? 8 If you are not disciplined (and everyone undergoes discipline), then you are illegitimate children and not true sons.

In an individual's attempt to live a disciplined life of faith and pursuit of God, both opposition and encouragement will come. Sometimes it is difficult to recognize the encouragement, since it can come in the form of the Lord's discipline.

Endure Opposition

3 Consider him who endured such opposition from sinful men, so that you will not grow weary and lose heart. 4 ¶ In your struggle against sin, you have not yet resisted to the point of shedding your blood.

The author again draws his readers attention to Jesus' death on the cross. That was the ultimate opposition from sinful men. The Hebrews are instructed to consider what Jesus went through and, therefore, not grow weary and lose heart.

Jesus endured verbal abuse, physical abuse, and even death. Individuals cannot feel sorry for themselves when they consider what Jesus endured. The fact that the readers are told: "You have not yet resisted to the point of shedding your blood" indicates that some might have to shed their blood. This is part of the cost of following Jesus. The ultimate resistance to sin is to believe in Jesus and be led by his indwelling Holy Spirit. This may well result in the persecution and death of the Hebrews who come to Jesus.

Be Encouraged by Discipline

5 And you have forgotten that word of encouragement that addresses you as sons: "My son, do not make light of the Lord's discipline, and do not lose heart when he rebukes you, 6 because the Lord disciplines those he loves, and he punishes everyone he accepts as a son." 7 Endure hardship as discipline; God is treating you as sons. For what son is not disciplined by his father? 8 If you are not disciplined (and everyone undergoes discipline), then you are illegitimate children and not true sons.

This section of the text makes a distinction between illegitimate children and true sons. The readers are told to be encouraged when they undergo hardship. It occurs because the Lord disciplines those he loves. The Lord's discipline is for the purpose of bringing his children to maturity. Discipline is sometimes easily identified as from the Lord; other times it might appear as opposition from sinful men. Discipline demonstrates that one is loved by the Lord and is accepted as a son.

The Hebrews would have less hardship if they rejected Jesus and attempted to remain under the old covenant. In that case, however, they would not be true sons, but illegitimate children. The true sons put their faith in Jesus and are subject to more hardship, chastening and discipline as proof of their relationship as sons.

Products of Discipline (12:9-11)

9 Moreover, we have all had human fathers who disciplined us and we respected them for it. How much more should we submit to the Father of our spirits and live! 10 Our fathers disciplined us for a little while as they thought best; but God disciplines us for our good, that we may share in his holiness. 11 No discipline seems pleasant at the time, but painful. Later on, however, it produces a harvest of righteousness and peace for those who have been trained by it.

Just as an earthly father disciplines his children, so also the heavenly Father disciplines his. When God the Father brings his children through difficult times it is to develop them into what he wants them to be. There are a number of products that come from the Lord's discipline.

Life

9 Moreover, we have all had human fathers who disciplined us and we respected them for it. How much more should we submit to the Father of our spirits and live!

Believers are reminded that an earthly father is respected when he properly disciplines his children. They are then instructed to submit to the discipline of their heavenly Father. The result of that discipline is life. One cannot truly live life to its fullest unless one submits to the Father's will, including his discipline.

Holiness

10 Our fathers disciplined us for a little while as they thought best; but God disciplines us for our good, that we may share in his holiness.

The heavenly Father is perfect and holy and desires his children to share in that holiness. Discipline is sometimes chosen by the father as the best way to produce holiness in his children.

Righteousness and Peace

11 No discipline seems pleasant at the time, but painful. Later on, however, it produces a harvest of righteousness and peace for those who have been trained by it.

The Hebrews are encouraged to endure painful and unpleasant discipline because it will produce a harvest of righteousness and peace. When discipline is allowed to train individuals, they will be at peace with God and in right standing with him. This is dealing with the area of fellowship with God. Only those walking in righteousness and peace may have true fellowship with God. Discipline has as one of its goals bringing about righteousness and peace.

Purpose of Discipline   (12:12-14)

12 Therefore, strengthen your feeble arms and weak knees! 13 "Make level paths for your feet," so that the lame may not be disabled, but rather healed. 14 Make every effort to live in peace with all men and to be holy; without holiness no one will see the Lord.

In light of the Lord's discipline a believer ought to see two effects in his life. He should be made strong and be able to live at peace with others.

Strength

12 Therefore, strengthen your feeble arms and weak knees! 13 "Make level paths for your feet," so that the lame may not be disabled, but rather healed.

Feeble arms, weak knees, and lameness are speaking metaphorically about one's spiritual walk. God's children can often be spiritually immature and weak. His discipline brings them strength so that they can run the race marked out for them.

Peaceful Living

14 Make every effort to live in peace with all men and to be holy; without holiness no one will see the Lord.

Peaceful living includes being at peace with God and at peace with man. Peace with God comes from walking in holiness. If one is living a holy life, he has taken a step to live at peace with man. Paul exhorts:

> "...as far as it depends on you, live at peace with everyone." (Rom 12:17)

Sometimes the holiest of people are opposed by sinful men. While an individual makes every effort to live at peace with those around him, the results of his efforts must be left with God.

Pitfalls of Discipline   (12:15)

15 See to it that no one misses the grace of God and that no bitter root grows up to cause trouble and defile many.

Sometimes amid discipline, a child of God may not see his loving hand in it. Since discipline by its nature is painful and unpleasant it can be misconstrued and thought of as evil. This could result in two common pitfalls.

Missing God's Grace

15 See to it that no one misses the grace of God

The grace of God is that which enables believers in Christ to do the Father's bidding. The goal of discipline is to bring God's children into conformity with his will. Discipline is therefore an act of God's grace as he deals lovingly with his children and brings them into conformity with his will. A pitfall would be to miss God's grace by perceiving discipline as something evil.

Becoming Bitter

and that no bitter root grows up to cause trouble and defile many.

Children who undergo significant discipline can become bitter. Paul informs fathers not to exasperate their children but to bring them up in the training and instruction of the Lord. (Eph 6:4) Earthly fathers can overdo or misuse discipline and cause bitterness to grow in their children.

This is not the case with the heavenly Father. His discipline is always perfect. One must resist allowing bitterness

265

to rear its ugly head, because it will cause trouble both for the person who is bitter and for many others who will be defiled by such bitterness.

Chapter Nineteen

Jesus is a Reason for
a Superior Kingdom (12:16 to 12:29)

An Example of Two Brothers (12:16-17)

16 See that no one is sexually immoral, or is godless like Esau, who for a single meal sold his inheritance rights as the oldest son. 17 Afterwards, as you know, when he wanted to inherit this blessing, he was rejected. He could bring about no change of mind, though he sought the blessing with tears.

Isaac's two sons, Jacob and Esau, serve as a contrast of the eternal and the temporal. Jacob was concerned with those things that were long term such as his inheritance rights and blessing. Esau, on the other hand, was concerned with those things that were immediate, such as satisfying his hunger. Esau is shown as an example of someone who will give up what is more valuable in the future for that which provides immediate gratification of needs.

A Birthright Forfeited

16 See that no one is sexually immoral, or is godless like Esau, who for a single meal sold his inheritance rights as the oldest son.

This section tells the Hebrews not to be sexually immoral or godless. Sexual immorality is not necessarily a reference to Esau. There is nothing in the Old Testament account to indicate that Esau was sexually immoral. Sexual immorality is an example of following a short-term desire.

Esau's problem is described as godlessness. The inheritance of the oldest son in Israel was more than just receiving twice the inheritance of the other children. It also meant being recognized as the leader of the home. In the case of Esau's sons, there was an additional right, and that was to be in the line of the Messiah. When Esau sold his inheritance rights for a bowl of soup, he showed how little he valued what God had planned. The fact is, the inheritance was not really Esau's to begin with. It had been promised to Jacob as part of the Lord's prophecy to Rebekah:

> The LORD said to her, "Two nations are in your womb, and two peoples from within you will be separated; one people will be stronger than the other, and the older will serve the younger." (Gen 25:23)

Although the inheritance was not Esau's to sell, his sale of it demonstrated how little he valued it.

The first-century Hebrews had the opportunity to inherit all the riches in Christ Jesus. Through the example of Esau, they are warned not to reject their inheritance for some temporal comfort. Their temptation is to reject Jesus as the Messiah and return to the Old Testament law. This would be more comfortable for them in the short run. The Romans were beginning to persecute Christians more aggressively, and fellow Jews were making it difficult for Christians, as well. Temporal comfort would come from remaining under the old covenant.

A Blessing Lost

17 Afterwards, as you know, when he wanted to inherit this blessing, he was rejected. He could bring about no change of mind, though he sought the blessing with tears.

Later in his life Esau wanted to be blessed by his father and sought that blessing with tears. Those tears came because he had lost something valuable. They were not tears of repentance. There was no change of heart in Esau. Instead he tried to get Isaac to change his mind.

God's children will be blessed by the Lord only when they recognize that their attitudes must be brought in line with his plan. Attempting to get God to change his mind and conform to their plan is futile.

An Example of Two Mountains   (12:18-24)

18 ¶ You have not come to a mountain that can be touched and that is burning with fire; to darkness, gloom and storm; 19 to a trumpet blast or to such a voice speaking words that those who heard it begged that no further word be spoken to them, 20 because they could not bear what was commanded: "If even an animal touches the mountain, it must be stoned." 21 The sight was so terrifying that Moses said, "I am trembling with fear." 22 But you have come to Mount Zion, to the heavenly Jerusalem, the city of the living God. You have come to thousands upon thousands of angels in joyful assembly, 23 to the church of the firstborn, whose names are written in heaven. You have come to God, the judge of all men, to the spirits of righteous men made perfect, 24 to Jesus the mediator of a new covenant, and to the sprinkled blood that speaks a better word than the blood of Abel.

The two mountains are used to represent the events of the issuing of the old covenant, as compared to the new covenant. The Hebrews are exhorted to see that they do not stand before Mount Sinai as their forefathers did but, instead, stand before Mount Zion. Mount Sinai represented a physical journey while Mount Zion represents a spiritual journey.

Mount Sinai

18 ¶ You have not come to a mountain that can be touched and that is burning with fire; to darkness, gloom and storm; 19 to a trumpet blast or to such a voice speaking words that those who heard it begged that no further word be spoken to them, 20 because they could not bear what was commanded: "If even an animal touches the mountain, it must be stoned." 21 The sight was so terrifying that Moses said, "I am trembling with fear."

Mount Sinai represents the Old Testament teaching about faith in a physical journey. The Israelite's journey was from the bondage of Egypt to freedom and rest in the promised land. The expressions used to describe Mount Sinai include "fire," "darkness," "gloom," "storm," "trumpets" and "voices." These are all an emphasis on things that are in the earth realm.

It was also described as a fearful assembly. Even Moses admitted that he was trembling with fear.

It was the place where the Israelites received the old covenant. This covenant was not able to bring life. Even Paul describes those under the old covenant as being under a curse (Gal 3:13). The physical faith journey from Egypt never resulted in the promised rest in the land.

Mount Zion

22 But you have come to Mount Zion, to the heavenly Jerusalem, the city of the living God. You have come to thousands upon thousands of angels in joyful assembly, 23 to the church of the firstborn, whose names are written in heaven. You have come to God, the judge of all men, to the spirits of righteous men made perfect, 24 to Jesus the mediator of a new covenant, and to the sprinkled blood that speaks a better word than the blood of Abel.

The Hebrews were told that they do not stand at Mount Sinai, rather at Mount Zion. In the first century, Mount Zion included Jerusalem and the temple mount. It was also used figuratively to represent heaven. It is the figurative usage utilized in this section. Mount Zion represents a spiritual journey from the bondage of law to freedom in Christ Jesus and the faith rest that comes in him.

Unlike the earthly events of Mount Sinai, Mount Zion represents heavenly events. It is described as the heavenly Jerusalem, the city of the living God.

It is not a fearful assembly, but it is described as a joyful assembly. Thousands upon thousands of angels are joining in this assembly. It is also described as an assembly of the firstborn. The word translated "church" is the Greek word "ekklesia" which means "assembly." Particularly when dealing with the Old Testament the translation "assembly" is preferred to the translation "church." The assembly of the firstborn is a reference to Exodus, chapter four, when the Lord instructed Moses what to say when he stands before Pharaoh:

> Then say to Pharaoh, 'This is what the LORD says: Israel is my firstborn son, and I told you, "Let my son go, so that he may worship me." But you refused to let him go; so I will kill your firstborn son.' " (Ex 4:22-23)

The writer to Hebrews concludes that the true spiritual Israelites are those who come to Mount Zion. They are the ones whose names are written in heaven. He describes them as righteous men made perfect. "Righteous men" is an apt description of the Old Testament saints trusting God and being saved by the promise of the coming Messiah. Being made perfect would be the result of Jesus sacrifice on the cross.

The author makes it clear that the way to "perfect" is Jesus, the mediator of a new covenant. Jesus' blood is better than all of the sacrifices that were made under the old covenant.

Jesus' blood speaks a better word then the blood of Abel. Abel's blood crying out from the ground represented condemnation and judgment. Jesus' blood represents sacrifice and forgiveness. Likewise, the old covenant brought judgment, while the new covenant brings freedom and rest.

An Example of Two Kingdoms   (12:25-29)

25 See to it that you do not refuse him who speaks. If they did not escape when they refused him who warned them on earth, how much less will we, if we turn away from him who warns us from heaven? 26 At that time his voice shook the earth, but now he has promised, "Once more I will shake not only the earth but also the heavens." 27 The words "once more" indicate the removing of what can be shaken—that is, created things— so that what cannot be shaken may remain. 28 Therefore, since we are receiving a kingdom that cannot be shaken, let us be thankful, and so worship God acceptably with reverence and awe, 29 for our "God is a consuming fire."

The contrast of the old covenant and the new covenant is now given in an example of two kingdoms. The old covenant represents an earthly kingdom which can be shaken and destroyed. The new covenant represents the unshakable kingdom of God.

The Shakable Kingdom of Man

25 See to it that you do not refuse him who speaks. If they did not escape when they refused him who warned them on earth, how much less will we, if we turn away from him who warns us from heaven? 26 At that time his voice shook the earth, but now he has promised, "Once more I will shake not only the earth but also the heavens." 27 The words "once more" indicate the removing of what can be shaken—that is, created things—so that what cannot be shaken may remain.

As in the previous verse, the one who speaks, described in verse 25, continues to be Jesus and his blood. The Hebrews are exhorted not to refuse Jesus. In making his point the author argues from the lesser to the greater. Those who were at Sinai were warned when God's voice shook the earth. Those at Mount Zion are able to hear the voice of Jesus who came from heaven to save his people Israel. If those at Sinai did not escape judgment, certainly those who know of Jesus' ministry will not escape judgment.

The earthly kingdom was never destined to last. It's destruction is described by John:

> Then I saw a new heaven and a new earth, for the first heaven and the first earth had passed away, and there was no longer any sea. I saw the Holy City, the new Jerusalem, coming down out of heaven from God, prepared as a bride beautifully dressed for her husband.(Rev 21:1-2)

It is also described by Peter:

> But the day of the Lord will come like a thief. The heavens will disappear with a roar;

the elements will be destroyed by fire, and
the earth and everything in it will be laid
bare. (2 Peter 3:10)

Isaiah mentions it, as well:

"Behold, I will create new heavens and a
new earth. The former things will not be
remembered, nor will they come to mind.
(Isaiah 65:17)

The kingdom of man on this earth is not eternal, but
only for a time.

The Unshakable Kingdom of God

*28 Therefore, since we are receiving a kingdom that cannot be
shaken, let us be thankful, and so worship God acceptably with
reverence and awe, 29 for our "God is a consuming fire."*

The Hebrews are again pointed to the wonderful opportunity before them to receive a kingdom that cannot be
shaken. They are exhorted to be thankful and to worship
God acceptably with reverence and awe. Acceptable
worship of God under the new covenant is to come to him
through faith in Jesus. To do anything less is to be an enemy
of God. For his enemies, God is a consuming fire. He will
consume those who do not come to faith in Jesus Christ.
The author of Hebrews makes a compelling argument
and expresses himself in terms that demonstrate his confidence that the Hebrews will make the right decision.

Chapter Twenty

Jesus is a Reason for Superior Living   (13:1 to 13:25)

Love People   (13:1-3)

1 ¶ Keep on loving each other as brothers. 2 Do not forget to entertain strangers, for by so doing some people have entertained angels without knowing it. 3 Remember those in prison as if you were their fellow-prisoners, and those who are ill-treated as if you yourselves were suffering.

Jesus has been presented as superior in every possible way. In this final chapter he is presented as a reason for superior living. On the basis of everything that has gone before, there is a way that believers ought to live. The readers are instructed how to live in relationship to other people.

Brothers

1 ¶ Keep on loving each other as brothers.

Chapter 13 begins with the Greek word "Philadelphia." It is composed of two root words. The first is "phileo," which means tender affections and the second is "adelphos" which means "brother" or literally "from the same womb." The fact that this exhortation is to "keep on loving" indicates that a love already existed. The word "brothers" refers to fellow Hebrews as opposed to Christians. The love of fellow Hebrews, who were from the common ancestry of Abraham, was already in existence. That is the love that was to continue.

By virtue of this letter, some of the Hebrews undoubtedly began following Jesus. This was not a reason to forsake their fellow Hebrews. They were to keep on loving them and hopefully lead them to faith in Jesus as the Messiah who had come.

Strangers

2 Do not forget to entertain strangers, for by so doing some people have entertained angels without knowing it.

The concept of loving people went beyond the Hebrew brothers. The writer exhorted his readers also to entertain strangers. Some might be fellow Hebrews, some might be Christians, some might be non-Christian Gentiles. It is a similar instruction to what Paul says to the Galatians:

> Therefore, as we have opportunity, let us do good to all people, especially to those who belong to the family of believers. (Gal 6:10)

Entertaining strangers in the Hebrew society included making meals for travelers or even inviting a guest into one's home overnight. There was not an abundance of inns or places to stay.

A reminder is given that sometimes angels can be the very strangers who are entertained. Hebrew readers would be likely to recount the entertaining of angels by Abraham:

> Abraham looked up and saw three men standing nearby. When he saw them, he hurried from the entrance of his tent to meet them and bowed low to the ground. He said, "If I have found favor in your eyes, my lord,

do not pass your servant by. Let a little water
be brought, and then you may all wash your
feet and rest under this tree. Let me get you
something to eat, so you can be refreshed
and then go on your way—now that you
have come to your servant." "Very well,"
they answered, "do as you say." (Gen 18:2-5)

Abraham eventually realized he was speaking to the
angel of the Lord and to other angels.

Even without the possibility of a stranger being an angel
there is still the certainty of Jesus teaching in the book of
Matthew:

"The King will reply, 'I tell you the truth,
whatever you did for one of the least of these
brothers of mine, you did for me.' (Matt
25:40)

Whenever a believer shows hospitality to others, he is
doing it unto the Lord.

Prisoners

*3 Remember those in prison as if you were their fellow-prison-
ers, and those who are ill-treated as if you yourselves were
suffering.*

The instructions concerning prisoners are an extension
of the golden rule:

So in everything, do to others what you
would have them do to you, for this sums up
the law and the Prophets. (Matt 7:12)

Believers are instructed to do for prisoners what they would hope someone might do for them if they were in prison. This would likely include visitation, financial help, care of family, and fervent prayer.

Avoid Sin (13:4-7)

4 Marriage should be honored by all, and the marriage bed kept pure, for God will judge the adulterer and all the sexually immoral. 5 Keep your lives free from the love of money and be content with what you have, because God has said, "Never will I leave you; never will I forsake you." 6 So we say with confidence, "The Lord is my helper; I will not be afraid. What can man do to me?" 7 Remember your leaders, who spoke the word of God to you. Consider the outcome of their way of life and imitate their faith.

The next series of exhortations for godly living deals with the subject of avoiding sin. Only a few sins are mentioned, but they are illustrative of the entire realm of sinfulness. The apostle John categorizes the things of this world, that we call sin, in his first letter:

> Do not love the world or anything in the world. If anyone loves the world, the love of the Father is not in him. For everything in the world—the cravings of sinful man, the lust of his eyes and the boasting of what he has and does—comes not from the Father but from the world. (1 John 2:15-16)

The cravings of sinful man is called lust of the flesh in the King James Version and could be shortened simply to lust. The lust of his eyes speaks of greed. The boasting of what he has and does refers to pride. These three categories of sin are sufficient for categorizing all sin that occurs.

Avoid Lust

4 Marriage should be honored by all, and the marriage bed kept pure, for God will judge the adulterer and all the sexually immoral.

This is a call to marital fidelity and sexual purity. God will condemn the adulterer, that is, the one who breaks his marriage vows. Likewise, he will condemn the sexually immoral, one who engages in sex without the benefit of marriage. Judgment of such activities often comes as broken homes, pregnancy, venereal disease, etc.

Although sex is the focus of this passage, lust comes in many other forms, including desires for alcohol, drugs, and overeating. All lust of the flesh is to be avoided.

Avoid Greed

5 Keep your lives free from the love of money and be content with what you have, because God has said, "Never will I leave you; never will I forsake you." 6 So we say with confidence, "The Lord is my helper; I will not be afraid. What can man do to me?"

The love of money speaks of greed. It is consistent with what Paul wrote to Timothy:

> For the love of money is a root of all kinds of evil. Some people, eager for money, have wandered from the faith and pierced them-selves with many griefs. (1 Tim 6:10)

Notice, in both texts it is not money that is the problem

but the love of money. It is not wrong to have money or even to be rich. Abraham, the father of these Hebrews, was extremely wealthy. Abraham, however, did not make his wealth his security. He depended on the Lord.

The text continues by encouraging contentment because God will never forsake his children. Just as with Abraham, the security of the Hebrews should be in the ever-abiding presence of the Lord. He is the one that will sustain them.

Avoid Pride

7 Remember your leaders, who spoke the word of God to you. Consider the outcome of their way of life and imitate their faith.

The word of God in the first century clearly included the message of Jesus as the Messiah. The leaders who spoke the Word of God would have to include that message or they would not be speaking God's word. Perhaps this would point them towards the apostles who were the leaders of the early church and who spoke boldly of Jesus. The outcome of their lives was to die for the sake of Jesus. In faith they followed Christ, regardless of persecution, ridicule, and severe suffering. They humbled themselves to become true followers of Jesus.

The Hebrews must also humble themselves and come to Jesus in faith. Pride often keeps people from coming to Christ. The faith of those, like the apostles and other leaders, is to be imitated because they put aside their pride and came to faith in Jesus as the Messiah who had come.

Learn Doctrine   (13:8-14)

8 Jesus Christ is the same yesterday and today and forever. 9 Do not be carried away by all kinds of strange teachings. It is good for our hearts to be strengthened by grace, not by ceremonial foods, which are of no value to those who eat them. 10 We have an altar from which those who minister at the tabernacle have no right to eat. 11 The high priest carries the blood of animals into the Most Holy Place as a sin offering, but the bodies are burned outside the camp. 12 And so Jesus also suffered outside the city gate to make the people holy through his own blood. 13 Let us, then, go to him outside the camp, bearing the disgrace he bore. 14 For here we do not have an enduring city, but we are looking for the city that is to come.

Coming to faith in Jesus as the Messiah results not only in loving people and avoiding sin but also in a desire to learn doctrine. Three specific areas are brought to mind, those of faith, grace and holiness.

Faith

8 Jesus Christ is the same yesterday and today and forever.

The readers were just exhorted to imitate the faith of their leaders. The basis for having that kind of faith is the fact that Jesus is the same yesterday, and today, and forever. Even though some of the nuances of faith change over time, the object of faith has always been the Messiah, who has now been identified as Jesus. The faith leaders of yesterday who were identified in Hebrews, chapter eleven, put their faith in the Messiah who was to come. The faith leaders of the first century were the apostles who put their faith in Jesus, the Messiah who had come. The faith leaders of tomorrow will be those who put their faith in the Messiah who had come and is coming again.

Grace

9 Do not be carried away by all kinds of strange teachings. It is good for our hearts to be strengthened by grace, not by ceremonial foods, which are of no value to those who eat them. 10 We have an altar from which those who minister at the tabernacle have no right to eat.

The strange teachings, referred to in this section, are not specifically identified. They involved ceremonial foods and sacrifices at an altar. It is quite likely that some were encouraging a faith in Jesus that included continuing the Jewish sacrificial system. This was a strange teaching in the sense that, once an all-sufficient sacrifice was made, no other sacrifice for sin existed. A clear choice must be made between those who minister at the tabernacle versus those who come to Jesus. Jesus has been characterized as the high priest, the temple veil, the sacrifice and now even the altar. Coming to Christ required leaving the old covenant. If one continued to minister at the tabernacle, he had no right to be part of Jesus.

Believers are to be strengthened by grace. The constant reflection on the goodness of Jesus in dying for the sins of mankind causes one to appreciate the grace of God. This is contrasted with attempts at pleasing God via daily sacrifices at the temple.

Holiness

11 The high priest carries the blood of animals into the Most Holy Place as a sin offering, but the bodies are burned outside the camp. 12 And so Jesus also suffered outside the city gate to make the people holy through his own blood. 13 Let us, then, go to him outside the camp, bearing the disgrace he bore. 14 For here we do not have an enduring city, but we are looking for the city that is to come.

The activity of the high priest is shown once again to be a shadow of what the reality is in Jesus. The high priest's carrying of the blood into the Most Holy Place was already shown to represent Jesus bringing his own blood into the Father's presence in heaven. The bodies of the animals that were sacrificed were then burned outside the camp. This depicted Jesus who would suffer outside the city gate. The purpose of his doing this was to make people holy through his own blood and sacrifice.

The Hebrews sought holiness by fulfilling the requirements of the sacrificial system at the temple in Jerusalem. Their sin was identified with the sacrificed animals. The writer to the Hebrews instructs them to find their holiness outside the camp by trusting in Jesus. They are no longer to identify with the animals on the altar but they should identify with Jesus and his suffering outside the city.

The temple located in the heart of Jerusalem was to be destroyed in a short time. The author reminded them that Jerusalem is not an enduring city. By going outside that city to Jesus, they look for a city that is to come. This is the same city Abraham was looking for:

> For he looked for a city which hath foundations, whose builder and maker [is] God.
> (Heb 11:10)

The earthly city would not long endure. The blood of animals had no value. The heavenly city is the one to be sought. The blood of Christ makes men holy and acceptable to God.

Worship God   (13:15-19)

15 Through Jesus, therefore, let us continually offer to God a sacrifice of praise—the fruit of lips that confess his name. 16 And do not forget to do good and to share with others, for with such sacrifices God is pleased. 17 Obey your leaders and submit to their authority. They keep watch over you as men who must give an account. Obey them so that their work will be a joy, not a burden, for that would be of no advantage to you. 18 ¶ Pray for us. We are sure that we have a clear conscience and desire to live honorably in every way. 19 I particularly urge you to pray so that I may be restored to you soon.

The old covenant and its sacrificial worship system was obsolete and aging and would soon pass away. The Hebrews were instructed in worship under the new covenant, which did not include the traditional activities of the temple. Instead of sacrifices of animals, this section speaks of sacrifices of praise and service.

Praise

15 Through Jesus, therefore, let us continually offer to God a sacrifice of praise—the fruit of lips that confess his name.

Jesus presented himself as the once-for-all sacrifice for sin. This event put an end to the sacrificial system at the temple. In this verse the author redefined sacrifice as praise which confesses his name. The way to praise God is to openly confess the name of Jesus.

In Hebrews 10 the father made it clear that he did not desire sacrifice and offering; rather he prepared a body for the Messiah. What pleased God was always his beloved Son, in whom he is well pleased. The Hebrews could only please God by confessing the name of Jesus. No worship of

God can exist apart from Jesus.

Service and Generosity

16 And do not forget to do good and to share with others, for with such sacrifices God is pleased.

Sacrifices were also identified with doing good and sharing with others. Jesus spoke of actions done to the least of these brothers of mine and identified them as actions done unto him. (Matt 25:40) Doing good for others at all times, and sharing material blessings, are sacrifices that are pleasing to God.

Obedience

17 Obey your leaders and submit to their authority. They keep watch over you as men who must give an account. Obey them so that their work will be a joy, not a burden, for that would be of no advantage to you.

The Lord has always placed a high priority on obedience. When Israel's first king, Saul, disobeyed the Lord's instructions by presenting offerings, the Lord sent the prophet Samuel with a message:

> But Samuel replied: "Does the LORD delight in burnt offerings and sacrifices as much as in obeying the voice of the LORD? To obey is better than sacrifice, and to heed is better than the fat of rams. (1 Sam 15:22)

Under the new covenant, sacrifices were no longer to be made but obedience was to continue.

The leaders, spoken of here, would be the very ones who

were presenting to them the message of Jesus. While the author of Hebrews might be a mystery to modern day readers, there is little doubt that the Hebrews knew who wrote the letter. This letter came to have Scriptural authority. Undoubtedly, there were other leaders who were accountable to God for their actions. The greatest joy that they could experience would be for these Hebrews to come to a saving knowledge of Jesus. Anything short of that would be a burden for the leaders and of no advantage to the Hebrews. Without confessing the name of Jesus, there is no salvation and, hence, no advantage to having received the message that Jesus is the Messiah who has come.

Prayer

18 ¶ Pray for us. We are sure that we have a clear conscience and desire to live honorably in every way. 19 I particularly urge you to pray so that I may be restored to you soon.

The request for prayer by the writer of Hebrews indicates that he was a leader of the people to whom he was writing. The fact that he uses the word "us" indicates that there were others that were part of his leadership team.

The writer's concern for a clear conscience has particular relevance to his delivering the truthful message about who Jesus is. Only by declaring the truth of the message God gave him would the writer of Hebrews have a clear conscience. It was not an easy message, but it was what the people needed to hear. His compassion for the people is demonstrated in his desire to be restored to them soon. He understands that their prayers could expedite this meeting.

Please Jesus   (13:20-25)

20 May the God of peace, who through the blood of the eternal covenant brought back from the dead our Lord Jesus, that great Shepherd of the sheep, 21 equip you with everything good for doing his will, and may he work in us what is pleasing to him, through Jesus Christ, to whom be glory forever and ever. Amen. 22 Brothers, I urge you to bear with my word of exhortation, for I have written you only a short letter. 23 I want you to know that our brother Timothy has been released. If he arrives soon, I will come with him to see you. 24 Greet all your leaders and all God's people. Those from Italy send you their greetings. 25 Grace be with you all.

This final section of superior living deals with doing the things that will please the Lord Jesus Christ. Jesus is pleased when he is the one that equips the believer for the purpose of helping others.

Let Jesus Equip You

20 May the God of peace, who through the blood of the eternal covenant brought back from the dead our Lord Jesus, that great Shepherd of the sheep, 21 equip you with everything good for doing his will, and may he work in us what is pleasing to him, through Jesus Christ, to whom be glory forever and ever. Amen.

These verses are a wonderful benediction that summarize what has been accomplished by God and his only begotten Son. He is described as the God of peace because he is the One who has allowed man to be at peace with God through his blood on the cross (Col 1:20). It is called the blood of the eternal covenant. This links together both the old covenant and the new. It demonstrates that God did not abandon one plan and start another plan, rather he planned all along that the old covenant would be replaced by the new. The blood of Christ was the only blood that would ever cause sins to be forgiven. No blood of animals would ever accomplish that. Through this eternal covenant, God brought back from the dead, Jesus.

The entire argument of Jesus/Messianic claim rests on the fact that he was raised from the dead. If he were still in the grave he could not be the king nor the high priest. His resurrection made Him high priest by the power of an indestructible life.

Jesus is described as that great shepherd of the sheep. This is a common expression for Jesus. Jesus used it himself, as recorded in the gospels. The prayer of this benediction is that believers will be equipped with everything they need to do God's will and please him through Jesus. Doing God's will is what pleases him and brings him glory. One can do God's will only when rightly related to Jesus and equipped by his spirit.

Help Others

22 Brothers, I urge you to bear with my word of exhortation, for I have written you only a short letter. 23 I want you to know that our brother Timothy has been released. If he arrives soon, I will come with him to see you. 24 Greet all your leaders and all God's people. Those from Italy send you their greetings. 25 Grace be with you all.

These final personal words are not a list of what believers ought to do, but they do show a level of concern believers should have for one another. The author is concerned with how his audience will receive his word of exhortation. He is concerned about Timothy, their brother. He has a desire to see these fellow Hebrews as soon as possible. He also sends them greetings from others who are with him in Italy, the likely place where the book was written.

The letter ends with a very simple but profound request to God. Grace be with you all.

Chapter Twenty-One

Jesus is the One Who was to Come
The Conclusion of Hebrews

Jesus is the Fulfillment of all Scripture
Concerning the Redeemer   (Luke 24:13-27)

The Old Testament promised a seed of the woman, a son of Abraham, a lion of Judah, a prophet like Moses, a king in David's line, a branch of the root of Jesse, a priest to minister forever, a rock to establish a nation and a Lord to reign forever. These and other promises like them clearly establish the fact that Old Testament saints were looking for a Messiah to come.

Jesus is the fulfillment of all those promises. The New Testament gives clear evidence of those who believe Jesus was the Messiah who was to come. These included John the Baptist, Joseph, the Magi, Mary, Simeon, Anna, Peter, and Jesus' disciples to name a few. These individuals moved their faith from the promise of a coming Messiah to the person of Jesus who was the Messiah who came.

Others alive at that time were continuing to believe in a coming Messiah but had failed to recognize that Jesus was the one. It was to this audience that the book of Hebrews was written in order to convince them of the authenticity of Jesus' Messianic claim. The author of Hebrews skillfully reviewed the history and practices of Judaism to demonstrate that Jesus was superior to and the fulfillment of these Old Testament experiences and practices.

He proves that Jesus is a superior message than any

brought by the prophets of the past. Jesus is superior to any of the angels that had been such a part of Hebrew understanding. He proves that Jesus brings the Sabbath rest that Joshua only hoped for. He shows that Jesus is a prophet like Moses and superior to Moses.

The author of Hebrews explained Jesus' priesthood under a new order, the order of Melchizedek. He showed that this Messianic priesthood is superior to the Aaronic priesthood in its appointment, teaching, hope, sanctuary, covenant, blood, and sacrifice. The eternal priesthood of Jesus the Messiah has replaced the temporary priesthood of Aaron and his descendants. A few years after the book of Hebrews was written the temple was destroyed and the Aaronic priesthood ceased to function. Even genealogical records to establish one's claim to priesthood were destroyed.

The author calls his Hebrew audience to leave the old covenant and its shadows and come instead to the new covenant and its reality of salvation through the blood of Jesus Christ, the Messiah who had come. Belief in Jesus would produce superior faith, superior saints, superior discipline, a superior kingdom and superior living.

The compelling drive of the author of Hebrews was to get his audience to have their sins forgiven and draw near to God by placing their faith in Jesus, the Savior, and Messiah. The testimony of Jesus is his indestructible life, as demonstrated by his resurrection from the dead. The Hebrew audience needed to receive Jesus as their Savior and Messiah.

The arguments of the book of Hebrews are no less compelling to today's reader. If one is trusting anything but Jesus for salvation and eternal destiny it is time to receive Jesus as personal Savior. Jesus is the one prophesied throughout the Old Testament, who came 2,000 years ago, and gave his life at Calvary for the sins of mankind. His resurrection has demonstrated his power over death. If individuals who have read this commentary are uncertain of their relationship to Jesus Christ, they should get on their knees, confess their sin, and ask Jesus Christ to save them.

Whether a first-century reader of the book of Hebrews or a 21st century reader of a commentary on Hebrews the most important decision of life concerns what one believes about Jesus. He is the Messiah; he is the one who was to come; he is the King; he will return soon!

Works Cited

Hughes, Philip Edgecumbe. <u>A Commentary on the Epistle to the Hebrews</u>. Grand Rapids: Eerdmans, 1977.

Josephus, Flavius. <u>The Wars of the Jews</u>. Grand Rapids: Baker Book House, 1979

MacArthur, John F. <u>The MacArthur New Testament Commentary, Hebrews</u>. Chicago: Moody, 1983.

alternate theory - Jesus &
    expelling of Christians from Rome

Judaism - a legal religion

Christianity - not ; attendance to synagogue as
                    replacement

Printed in the United States
963500002B

9 781591 605317